Stephen Bruyant-Langer

The Personal Business Plan

A blueprint for running your life

WILEY

Cover design by Salad Creative Ltd

Registered office
John Wiley and Sons Ltd, The Atrium, Southern Gate, Chichester, West Sussex, PO19 8SQ,
United Kingdom

For details of our global editorial offices, for customer services and for information about how to
apply for permission to reuse the copyright material in this book please see our website at www.
wiley.com.

Wiley publishes in a variety of print and electronic formats and by print-on-demand. Some
material included with standard print versions of this book may not be included in e-books or in
print-on-demand. If this book refers to media such as a CD or DVD that is not included in the
version you purchased, you may download this material at http://booksupport.wiley.com. For
more information about Wiley products, visit www.wiley.com.

Designations used by companies to distinguish their products are often claimed as trademarks.
All brand names and product names used in this book and on its cover are trade names, service
marks, trademark or registered trademarks of their respective owners. The publisher and the
book are not associated with any product or vendor mentioned in this book. None of the
companies referenced within the book have endorsed the book.

Library of Congress Cataloging-in-Publication Data is available

A catalogue record for this book is available from the British Library.

ISBN 978-1-118-74413-0 (hardback)   ISBN 978-1-118-74424-6 (ebk)
ISBN 978-1-118-74425-3 (ebk)

Set in 10/14.5 pt Palatino LTStd by Toppan Best-set Premedia Limited

Printed and Bound in the United Kingdom by TJ International Ltd., Padstow, Cornwall.

To Mette, Caroline, Claudia, Amanda and Adam.

Thank You for Everything.

CONTENTS

LIST OF FIGURES AND TABLES IN
THE PERSONAL BUSINESS PLAN

INTRODUCTION
WHAT CAN I USE *THE PERSONAL BUSINESS PLAN* FOR?

> *"* Take a chance
> while you still got the choice *"*
> *AC/DC*

Life has taught me that you need an overarching life ambition in order to succeed. You need to remain learning agile in order to be able to reinvent yourself. And you need to have the courage to commit yourself in order to be happy.

Throughout my career as a headhunter I have had the privilege of interviewing and coaching thousands of outstanding leaders. These trustful dialogues with resourceful leaders have taught me a great deal about success in business and success in life. I would like to share some of the key findings to help you identify the personal and career paths which will make you successful.

My approach to both personal and professional life is that if you can dream it, you can do it. But in the necessary soul-searching process you must be ready to look the monster in the eye: The monster in this case being the sum of your self-limitations. Throughout your life you have constructed a truth about who you are; this truth limits you in the exploration and utilization of new experiences that could disrupt this idea. In turn, this self-imposed limitation means that you stop learning. There is no Truth with a capital T.

In your professional life it is important to know your adversary and to recognize that sometimes you can be your own "worst enemy". You need to liberate and enable yourself, and become Pinocchio with no strings to tie you down. You need not lie – least of all to yourself. The feeling is great – to feel free and be able to focus on the future.

In my experience, most executives have great difficulties in applying their professional toolbox and techniques to their personal lives. Many – in fact most – mention one of the following existential dilemmas and challenges:

⊗ How do I balance my professional life and my personal life?
⊗ How do I get the most out of my high potential situation?
⊗ How do I create a sustainable position for my family and myself in this volatile, uncertain, complex and ambiguous world?
⊗ How do I identify and focus on the important things in life?
⊗ How do I avoid the emotional burnout that results from constantly giving to others?
⊗ How do I find happiness?

I have come to realize that our most secret thoughts are also the most common. These questions and thoughts are the reasons why I have chosen to write this book.

The Personal Business Plan will help you answer these fundamental questions and help you survive, live, and thrive. I have known leaders who have lost themselves in success – who have derailed and have fallen into the abyss of stress, substance abuse, addiction, divorce, depression, or suicide. The need to make the most of your strengths without overdoing them – without derailing – seems to be more relevant in the twenty-first century than ever before. You must reduce the risks in your personal life in order to perform in business life – and vice versa. I'll help you find your own way through the labyrinth – becoming maze bright and organizationally savvy. My mission in life is to make you happier.

The **Four-Leaf Clover** has become my signature. By using this core concept you will experience the different parts of your life falling into place. You will obtain a clear picture of your existential platform and you will improve your life. You will be able to act it out by turning thoughts into action – and action into value.

I will enable you to establish your own Four-Leaf Clover model which will document how each of the actions in your life fits into the greater picture and makes you develop your strengths and grow. You will have a strong sense of cross-fertilization between the different areas in your life and, as a direct consequence, you will become more self-aware and robust. Self-awareness and experience build resilience.

Figure 1 The Four-Leaf Clover

A business plan is a well-known concept in business. An ambitious business plan has many qualities. It is precise, it is complete and it is specific. It relates both to the short run and to the long run. First and foremost it can be executed. At thepersonalbusinessplan.com you will find a goldmine of resources in the form of tools, techniques, templates, cases, examples and exercises – together with articles, interviews and videos detailing the research behind *The Personal Business Plan*. I have also included my 10 best pieces of good advice:

Inspiration: How to Obtain Success and Happiness

1. Be generous
2. Be inclusive and tolerant
3. Stop living up to other people's expectations
4. Be an interesting conversation partner
5. Be direct and consequent in your communication
6. Spend 10 000 hours on becoming excellent at something
7. Break the mold before you break down
8. Run a risk from time to time
9. Find your life ambition
10. Reinvent yourself

The Personal Business Plan is the central tool in the executive coaching system I have been perfecting since 1996. Since then I have had the privilege of contributing significantly to breakthroughs for thousands of executives undergoing periods of personal transition. They have carried through the same steps and answered the same questions that I will ask you to reflect on over the following pages. For everybody, it has led to fundamental improvements in their lives. *The Personal Business Plan* allows you to perform judicious pivotal shifts around a fixed starting point: your values. It gives you renewed flexibility and certainty in your personal choices. As a dynamic document it offers you the opportunity for ongoing documentation of and building on your life experiences.

Most of the time, we have difficulties making important personal decisions. It is much easier for us to make decisions about something which doesn't directly affect our own emotions or our own future. I remember a very successful CEO who told me that he had never himself taken any fundamentally existential decision. He had simply followed the flow. And now he felt a void. When you make personal choices you also discard personal opportunities and that is very difficult for most people. It seems risky not to keep open all potential scenarios. Have the courage to commit yourself. Please remember that history never shows the alternative. You will be rewarded for making decisions – the right decisions.

When we have finally made a tough decision, then we are often good at executing it. Once you have decided what you want with your life, then you can plan the work as linearly as you plan any other project. It is the "what" which is difficult, not the "how". You are used to solving problems: It is much more challenging for you to make an existential decision about "where" to go than executing the plan, once you have made it. The steps then are often self-evident. The perplexity and the doubt – everything that lures you into delaying instead of acting – exist because you still lack answering some fundamental questions about your life situation, your life ambition and your dreams.

I have come to believe more and more that, in order to perform as a trusted advisor and participate in the changing careers and lives of highly qualified professionals, I need to be able to create an inner space from where I can draw energy when needed. The success of an intervention depends on the interior condition of the intervener. The quality and character of this interior condition is at the heart of leadership success.

Let's assume that this book contains the answers that you are looking for.

What Was Your Question?

This question says more about yourself than nearly anything else you may formulate to yourself. You need a framework – a guiding principle – to help you in your endeavors. In essence *The Personal Business Plan* is an answer to all central questions around you. When you have finished the book you will have formulated "the business plan of your life".

Goals are dreams with deadlines. *The Personal Business Plan* turns your dreams and aspirations into specific and measurable targets. It's a compass which will help you choose when you find yourself bewildered and don't know which way to go. It teaches you your life patterns and helps you break them when necessary. It will be a valuable tool for you whenever you need to reflect upon or make decisions about your career and your life. If you take this process seriously it will in itself create exceptional value for you.

In the old days – that is, yesterday – there was the Peter Principle, which asserted that employees would continue to be promoted until they reached their level of incompetence. Today's workplace has ushered in a new principle; it's called the *Paul Principle*. The Paul Principle states that employees don't need to get promoted to become incompetent. They will become incompetent in their current jobs if they don't grow, adapt, and evolve.[1]

The important message is: "I need to change". And you are not alone. We all need to change in order to succeed in life. I call it serial mastery: When you've become excellent at something, then it's time to reinvent yourself. There are no traffic jams along the extra mile.

And the simple fact that I live, work, and thrive in Denmark – consistently the happiest country (or one of the happiest countries) in the world[2] – should make you feel at ease. I know what good looks like!

The former Chinese president Hu Jintau, when visiting Denmark, said: "This is luxury". He explained his spontaneous exclamation the following way:

> *//* Look at the people and how they take the time to sit and have a beer or a cup of coffee with their friends and family. And breathe the air and feel how crisp and fresh it is. If we can bring this from Denmark to the Chinese people, they would be much happier than they are today.[3] *//*

One of the main reasons for the quality of life in Denmark is not visible to the eye. It is trust: Trust in the institutions, trust in others, and trust in yourself. There is also a certain paradox associated with trust. You may have a specific trust in your bank but a generalized mistrust regarding the financial sector. In Denmark equality is high (measured by the Gini coefficient), delegation is high, average income is high, taxation is high, digitalization is high, educational level is high. Furthermore pollution is low, crime is low, corruption is low, unemployment is low, distances are small, traffic is smooth, and public transport is effective. Finally, relationships are predominantly collaborative, cooperative, and interactive. All of this fosters a climate of general wellbeing and balance. Add to this inspiring talent within gastronomy, art, music, architecture, and design, and you get a higher quality of life overall.

Just for the record: I am not complacent. I am acutely aware of global competition and that the European welfare model may not be sustainable. I often half-jokingly say that, in Asia you tend to work as long as in Europe, you simply start eight hours earlier. There is no doubt that the geopolitical balance is shifting towards Asia and that the rising social costs in Europe represent a time bomb under the system.

Instruction

It is important for me that the well-documented and time-tested framework of *The Personal Business Plan* leads to action for you and makes you succeed in your endeavors, just as it has for so many other life ambitious individuals.

Toolkit

At thepersonalbusinessplan.com you will find your clean *Personal Business Plan Toolkit*. Download it – but don't read ahead. You will get enough to think about over the course of the book and answering one question at a time. You will also find your clean *Personal Business Plan Toolkit* at the end of this book.

How is This Book Structured?

When reading through the chapters you will experience consistency. I have focused on making the questions and the exercises as simple and precise as possible. Each of the 10 chapters consists of a set of three existential questions.

1. What Is My Situation?

This is where you define the baggage that you carry around and that you have to let go of. This is what we are setting out to do. Together we define your **Four-Leaf Clover**, your life's stepping stones, which together form the basis of your life-long learning. In the definition of your potential, you will begin to find clarity and comfort. Actually, you knew it already, but nobody has ever challenged you to express it as transparently. Don't try to satisfy an imaginary public – do what makes you happy! Change the conversation.

2. How Can I Thrive?

We establish your internal wellbeing benchmark. What does it mean when you say that you feel good? Compared to what? We go through a **Heaven and Hell Exercise** which forces you chronologically to compare for example the happiness of succeeding in high school or being promoted at work to the sorrow of a divorce or a child being ill. Together we define your life anchors and look for situations where there is an alignment between your interests, competencies, and possibilities. We establish your talents, knowledge, and capabilities.

3. When Do I Perform at My Best?

Now we focus on your professional life. Together we establish the conditions that make you thrive in your work life – your **Functional Condition Map**. This means that you get to calibrate what is important to you from a career perspective. Some drivers are universal, but you have something which specifically motivates you more than anything else and define what sustained success means to you. You need to transcend your self-perception and work hard to become the best version of yourself.

4. What Energizes Me?

In order to make the best of your future, we must now work with your key competencies. We will distill your passion and leverage your strengths while damage controlling your weaknesses. You will produce a **Personal SWOT Analysis** defining your strengths, weaknesses, opportunities, and threats, and identify the challenges that will enable you to make an epic win. Live a life that truly looks like you. It is your responsibility to remain relevant.

5. Where am I on My Personal Journey?

This is where we determine which phase of your life you are at. What are your priorities in life? What is your potential for personal growth? In principle we are all living the same life. We go through the same seasons and we have the same preoccupations. Research has defined a generic life phase and the book will introduce you to the most important **Life Phase Analysis**. Why not learn the guiding principles that can help you get the best out of your life? Why not piggyback on other people's experiences?

6. How Do I Become Happy?

We all share some basic needs and aspire to some inherently human characteristics of happiness. The central question is: What are you looking for? The concept of **Happiness 360** will be used to identify the stakeholders of your life and identify their expectations. How does this concept of Happiness 360 influence your feeling of wellbeing and how will the insight benefit you and make you an even better leader? You need to surprise both others and yourself.

7. How Do I Reinvent Myself?

Of course there is no such thing as a free lunch. You will need to decide what you are willing to sacrifice. Actually you don't need to sacrifice anything; you simply need to make choices. At this point you will have a firm grip on your life ambition, and this concept will serve you as a helpful guideline. Your reinvention is not easy, you will need help from good people, and luckily for you they are out there – it's simply a question of asking for help.

8. How Do I Differentiate Myself from Others?

The fundamental idea here is to find out how you stand out from others and what you are better at than anybody else. If you want to stand out you need to be outstanding. You don't need to compete with others. Make them irrelevant – compete only with yourself. How good do you want to be? If you stick your nose out then of course there is a risk of failure. Learn to dominate that fear and live with a fundamental trust in your future.

9. What Is My Personal Business Plan?

Finally you have reached a higher level by documenting how to reinvent yourself and remain relevant. Through hard work you have made and written your own Personal Business Plan. Your attitude and mindset have changed. You know your **BATNA (Best Alternative To Negotiated Agreement)**.[4] Your personal choices are more grounded than ever and you are seen as a person in balance with yourself and your surroundings. You feel more authentic. You are able to create personal meaning and dare to be yourself – it is fundamental to the quality of your life. You are ready and set to go for your life ambition.

10. What Have I Learned?

As you reach the end of the book, you'll be asked: What is your key learning? What energizes you and gives you a feeling of flow? Through **Scenario Writing** you will be able to decide exactly along which course you want to progress. By documenting a process you commit yourself to the project. So reflection leads to documentation. And from here action is a natural next step. Disregard some of the advice given to you earlier on in your life and career – you have probably already evolved so significantly and improved so much that the advice is no longer relevant. Now, if you were sure not to fail, what would you do?

Onwards and upwards!

"It is the possibility of having a dream come true that makes life interesting." This quote from the Brazilian author Paulo Coelho is my favorite quote. It is worthwhile pursuing your dream. Much too often we lack the imagination necessary to comprehend how much we can fulfill in the one life we have at our disposal. When you have reached a situation where you spend your time on tasks which you consider meaningful, which are fun and which give you energy instead of draining you then you will never look back, then you've reached a tipping point, and you will instinctively direct your thoughts towards the future.

Inspiration: A Real Life Example

Some years ago I was contacted by a man named Niels Moller Nielsen who wanted to discuss his life situation and his development as a top executive in the telco industry. He worked as Nokia's CEO in Ukraine and had organized his work life according to his priorities, not least to keep the close contact to his son. In Kiev his base was a hotel room. Every second Wednesday he flew to Denmark in order to spend time together with his son and on Monday morning he drove his son to school on the way to the airport. Back in Ukraine he then focused on work and was present and visible vis-à-vis his 80 employees.

However, there was also a dissonance. Niels described himself as a fiery person and the more questions I asked him to reflect on the clearer my picture became. "You remind me of a Formula 1 driver who barely keeps the car in the curves without skidding", I told him the first time we met and he perfectly understood what I meant. Maybe time had come to view himself more as a *gray eminence* and strive for more *boardroom appearance* – to radiate overview and exude a natural authority. We continued to meet, talking about his way from elementary school to the job as CEO of Nokia Russia, which he got after Ukraine with P&L responsibility for several billion dollars. It very soon became clear to me that Niels Moller Nielsen as a leader was exceptionally focused.

Focus has two functions – a laser function and a filter function – and both provide energy. The laser function seeks out the central issues and the filter function sorts out the rest. The choices he had made in his private life had given him a sense of balance and now he wanted the same sense of balance in his professional life. He had created a greater distance to his surroundings and employees than he wanted – and he could clearly see it himself. We spoke about many things that he could do differently when returning to Kiev.

Already the third time we met I was happy to be able to tell him: "You seem much more at ease and much more relaxed". He then told me that he could clearly sense how others had begun to see him as a more whole person – more spacious and judicious. By gradually opening up and showing some vulnerability Niels Moller Nielsen felt stronger than ever.

Throughout the book, you will find the story of Flemming Borreskov, the former CEO of Realdania, the most influential philanthropic foundation in Denmark. He is on version 7.0 of himself and will be one of our heroes in this tale. Flemming Borreskov has carried out all the exercises and answered all the questions in his Personal Business Plan. Thanks to applying this mental discipline he has succeeded in taking control of his life and his future. He is a perfect example of the power of *The Personal Business Plan* and a role model in planning his life.

I SALUTE HIM!

I have also included the story of Jan Asmussen who is at an earlier stage in his life than Flemming Borreskov. He works as a Nordic Controller at the Nordic Headquarter of CSC, one of the largest IT solution providers in the world. He is a wise man who has successfully dealt with his main challenge, namely that he is profoundly introvert. In that respect, his Personal Business Plan complements that of Flemming, who is resolutely extrovert. An extremely interesting fact is that many successful senior executives are indeed introverts, who use their time and energy on solving issues rather than rising and shining. If you are, yourself, an introvert, Jan's story will give you deep insights into dealing with the potential downsides and optimize your behavior in order to get as much credit as possible. If you are, yourself, an extrovert, you will learn what a valuable personality trait introversion can be. Western society in general promotes and rewards extroversion. However, introversion might provide the key to what is worth being extrovert about!

I SALUTE HIM!

In any case the dichotomy between the two tales will allow you to compare and contrast. It will also allow you to comprehend how flexible the Personal Business Plan framework is. It has been used successfully by students, housewives, and the self-employed, as well as middle managers, directors, and senior executives. The mindset behind is existential – therefore it also applies to you.

Flemming's Tale: The Making of *The Personal Business Plan*

Flemming Borreskov made a personal commitment to himself early on. He wanted to leave at the top of his game. He had seen too many CEOs of prominent companies going into retirement and vanishing into oblivion. And in order to be able to carry through his promise he needed a compelling life ambition. What did he discover? He found out that there was one thing he had never done. He had been a marketing director, he had been a sales director and he had been a CEO. He had worked in the public sector, he had worked in the private sector, and he had worked in a philanthropic foundation; but he had never had his own company! I will never forget the glimpse of boyish charm and joy that passed over the face of this noble man in his sixties when he, in his core, realized that this was what he was going to do for the rest of his working life. Found a company together with his wife and build up a totally new existence based on his fundamental values – a company centered round catalytic society.

Jan's Tale: A High Performer with High Potential

Jan Asmussen had made significant choices in his life. When he had found himself at a dead end he had always created his way out – often by taking a path which might at first seem risky. He had always landed solidly on his feet – quietly and robustly he had managed personal and professional transitions. Before joining CSC he was a Partner in two global auditing companies, Grant Thornton and BDO. He deeply felt a need to leave the hamster wheel and actively contribute by personally implementing business solutions instead of being limited to auditing. His journey is the journey of a specialist developing into a generalist – a business oriented leader. This reliable and trustworthy man in his early forties also deeply felt that he lacked some inspiration in his daily life. Therefore he had come to me for guidance. As he succinctly pointed out in one of our early sessions: "The future belongs to those who believe in the beauty of their dreams". My interpretation was that Jan was looking for life quality.

What Do *You* Do?

Many people find it tiring to meet the same question over and over at receptions and family parties and other places where people meet:

"So, what about you, what do *you* do?"

I don't feel like that. I love that question. Many years ago I decided to perceive this question as a challenge. As a chance to present my professional life in a way that creates interest and might be the spark to a giving dialogue. Which forces me to put words on what I think is important.

My answer is often:

"I change lives."

To create change in other people's lives sounds somewhat more exciting than "I recruit executives". And when I suggest that I change lives, it's for real. As a senior partner in Korn/Ferry International, the world's largest executive recruiting firm and a leading global provider of talent management solutions, I help top management of the world's largest companies reach their objectives. Korn/Ferry International places nine professionals into new roles every hour. I am used to treating personal and corporate information confidentially – as one of my candidates once told me: "I could tell you more, but then I'd have to kill you!"

The core in my work is the insightful dialogue. Both as a headhunter and as an executive coach I find myself working in the boundary between psychology and business. I have worked for more than 17 years in executive search and spent a number of these years together with some of the best business psychologists. Before that I worked 15 years as Marketing Director for L'Oréal and The Coca-Cola Company. Over the past 17 years I have also taught at Copenhagen Business School as an External Lecturer in Strategic Market Management and Corporate Communication.

Everything I write is based on research and more than 17 years of experience helping career people find their own way. At Korn/Ferry International we always work on a scientific foundation and much of our new knowledge is published at kornferryinstitute.com. Korn/Ferry International has assessed more than 1 million candidates. I have personally carried out more than 6000 candidate interviews and placed more than 700 executives.

So when I say that I change lives, then it's true. Not sometimes, but every time. The reason why I can be so convinced is that I've seen it thousands of times and continue to receive many testimonials from people who are grateful that they have followed *The Personal Business Plan*. In short my mission is to make you happier.

Inspiration: Personal Reinventions

The *Bill & Melinda Gates Foundation* is the largest transparently operated private foundation in the world. The primary aims of the foundation are, globally, to enhance healthcare and reduce extreme poverty, and in America, to expand educational opportunities and access to information technology. There is a direct line between the individual (Bill Gates), the group (the foundation), the organization (the projects) and society (healthcare, poverty, education, and IT). Therefore it intuitively makes sense. And the intriguing dimension behind this tale is that it allows Bill Gates to reinvent himself from being the person who made the most money in the world to becoming the person who gave the most money in the world.

Al Gore served as the 45th Vice President of the United States (1993–2001), under President Bill Clinton. He was the Democratic Party's nominee for President and lost the US presidential election in 2000 despite winning the popular vote. Gore is currently an author and environmental activist. He has founded a number of non-profit organizations, including the Alliance for Climate Protection, and has received the Nobel Peace Prize for his work in climate change activism. Again there is a direct line between the individual (Al Gore), the group (environmentalists), the organization (the non-profit organizations) and society (climate change). And this process has allowed Al Gore to reinvent himself from being a former US presidential candidate to becoming a global frontrunner within environmental causes.

Bill Clinton left office with the highest end-of-office approval rating of any US president since World War II. Since then, he has been involved in public speaking and humanitarian work. Based on his philanthropic worldview, Clinton created the William J. Clinton Foundation to promote and address international causes such as prevention of AIDS and global warming. In 2004, he published his autobiography *My Life* and in 2007, he published *Giving: How Each of Us Can Change the World*. This is another clear example of a spectacular reinvention from being president to becoming an advocate for global philanthropy. Again we see a clear connection between the individual (Bill Clinton), the group (the foundation), the organization (the projects), and society (AIDS and global warming). He once confided that he had made a specific plan after being re-elected for his second term – however, at that time he didn't know about *The Personal Business Plan*. There is no limit to what you can do if you prepare yourself properly and have the courage to commit yourself entirely.

What I Expect from You

Maybe you are a leader, maybe you are an ambitious employee climbing the corporate ladder or maybe you work in a public organization. It really doesn't matter. In any case, this book puts some demands on you:

- ❖ You must be open and show trust
- ❖ You must perceive joy of life as important
- ❖ You must have ambitions
- ❖ You must have the will to look yourself in the eye

The important thing is that you are motivated to make decisions about your life and ready to take the consequence of these decisions. Perhaps the most fundamental prerequisite for you is even more pragmatic:

"Don't declare, deliver".

If you don't meet the success criteria in your present job you need to find out what is missing. This book will help you act and create a context in which you will succeed. And the road to success is at the same time inspirational, tough, energizing and rewarding.

I would like to point out a few ground rules:

The process needs to take time. My recommendation is that you spend a minimum of one week on each of the 10 steps and that you give yourself a minimum of one hour to answer each of the 30 questions – and preferably a lot longer to reflect upon each of them. During the program you will find different exercises that take several hours.

The process requires calmness. If you answer the questions sit on the sofa with the television on and the children playing loudly around you then you might as well leave it. The end result becomes much stronger when you are able to reflect and listen to your feelings and thoughts.

Just write along. There is no "right" way to fill out your Personal Business Plan and the most important receiver of it is yourself. Nor is there a correct extent of the final document – however, it often boils down to around 25 pages. If you feel the need to digress then you can always make an appendix where you park your thoughts and ideas which are not directly related to your present and future life situation.

The Personal Business Plan is iterative. This means that you, while completing it, are free to go back and re-evaluate the answers you gave in the light of your subsequent answers and reflections. This is particularly crucial when you have answered the last question. At that point in time it is important that you edit and write through the document in order to keep the red thread.

The earlier in life you adhere to the life philosophy behind *The Personal Business Plan* the happier you will become.

Fundamentally, the form of the book is everything that you should aim to be. Ambitious. Energetic. Challenging. Clear. Positive.

On their death bed people don't talk about what they did – they talk about what they didn't do. My objective is that this book gives you a wake-up call. You decide much more than you think you do. The field is much bigger than you believe. In the best of worlds this book will motivate you to reach for your dreams, and when you have found the way you will say to yourself: "I cannot *not* do this!"

Probably, you will experience that the road is quite different from what you believed. Because even though there is plenty of specific advice in this book it is the *questions* which are most important. An AESC (Association of Executive Search Consultants) survey taken some years ago found that most people spend more time planning their annual vacation than they do planning their career![5]

Your Life Platform

A way of illustrating your life platform is by using the Venn diagram.[6] Typically used in mathematics, the Venn diagram shows all the possible relationships

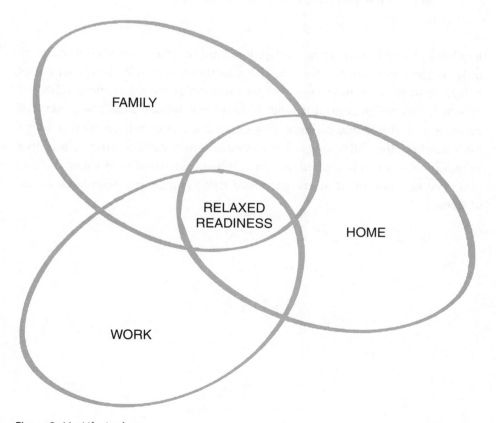

Figure 2 My Life Anchors

among various different sets of abstract objects. In the overlapping section of the following sets of three circles lies the key to truly understanding yourself.

My *Golden Rule of Life Anchors* is: Don't change more than two at the same time! During your life multiple changes will occur in the three different spheres. A possible scenario is that you will get married, you will have kids, you will move several times, you will have many jobs and you also may divorce. On top of that illness and existential crises will contribute to the turbulence.

When considering your options, think of them in pairs. For example:

- Don't make a big family decision if at the same time you are getting a new job.
- Don't change your job if you are having a family crisis.
- Don't move if you have just gotten a new job.
- And so on.

Inevitably, these events often overlap, for example when you need to move in order to get a new job and there is also a tendency for multiple opportunities to turn up at the same time. However, try to minimize the simultaneous changes of which you are in control. I would like to put *Relaxed Readiness*, a state of awareness, as the central common element of these three spheres; that is, in the middle where they all overlap. Sometimes you may need to take a deep dive in order to use a window of opportunity. When confronted with major choices, you need not feel stifled by the perceived risks; you simply need to be aware of them.

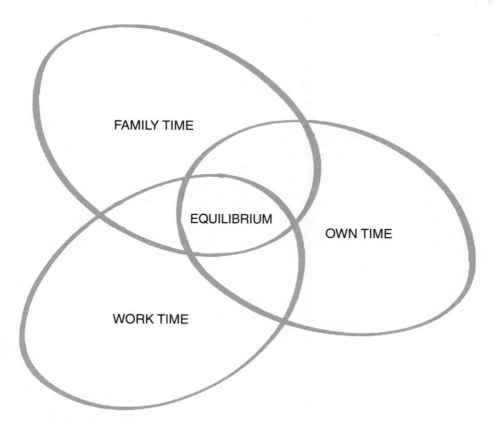

Figure 3 The Importance of Time

There is an inherent conflict in these three time perspectives. In the overlap is "Equilibrium", but very seldom you will find yourself in this hot spot. During a lifetime much time goes with the "production" associated with raising a family and working. So there is seldom much time left as "Own time". This time, however, is primordial for regenerative purposes. Time where you reap what you have sown. So much time goes with production that we hardly remember why we are so productive. Well, the answer is: "To enjoy ourselves!"

I can promise you two things:

If you approach your career as professionally as you approach your tasks then you will be successful. If you approach your life as professionally then you will become happy. Self-observation will lead to self-awareness. By documenting your behavior and your dreams you will progressively align the two and prioritize the actions that lead you towards your ultimate goal.

1

What is My Situation?

*I'm taking control of my life –
now, right now*
Tom Petty

We all experience forced choices and there seems to be a built-in urge to organize the world in opposites. Are you verbally or numerically oriented? Does your company focus on innovation or efficiency? What is most important for you – your career or your family life?

Juxtapositions are destructive, because they always create a false picture of reality. If you aim at a harmonious life where you balance different dimensions according to your life ambition, then juxtapositions are decidedly lethal. Each and every time you create a schism inside your head you must try to reposition and challenge yourself. This is valid not least for so-called "soft" and "hard" values. If you find yourself in a situation where you feel you have to choose between prioritizing the hard and the soft values in your life, then you will fail. You should always be in a position to identify a meta-level and think of a solution that transforms the schism into a "both/and" situation, allowing you to transcend trade-offs. A Japanese proverb says: *Vision without action is a daydream – action without vision is a nightmare.*

Just in order to name a few resolutions of dilemmas:

⊗ You must pursue both professional and personal ambitions in order to create an optimal career – look for your life ambition.
⊗ You must focus on both your intellectual and your spiritual competencies in order to leave a mark – look for your energizers.

⊗ You must focus on both the present and the future, that is, both short-term and long-term in order to create wellbeing – look for what will ultimately make you happy.

⊗ You must focus on both the vision and the operation, that is, both strategy and implementation in order to succeed – look for what differentiates you from others.

When you find yourself in situations where you have to choose between two paths always ask yourself: Is it possible to find a third way where I don't need to opt out on either A or B? My experience is that C exists. Should I accept this job or should I ask for a higher salary? You could combine the two, state that you are highly interested and want to negotiate a bonus based on clear success criteria. In reality there are very few opposites. You don't need to be either a tough or an inclusive employer. You might choose to be tough on tasks and soft on people. My experience from CEOs in all weight classes is that, the longer along their life, the more they perceive dilemmas from a holistic point of view. Their perspective becomes more inclusive and participative.

The leadership styles of senior executives are the complete opposite of lower-level managers' styles. The *decisive style*, which combines the use of minimal information and a single option, is dominant among first-level supervisors but nearly non-existent among senior executives. Similarly, the fast-moving, multi-focused *flexible style*, embraced by senior executives, scored lowest among supervisors.

The *hierarchic style* (lots of data, one option) is the second-most frequently used for first-line supervisors; its use dips during a manager's career and bounces back somewhat at the most senior level. And the integrative style, relied on so heavily by senior executives, ranks near the bottom for junior managers (see Figure 4A).

At the second level of management, the scores are tightly clustered with no one style dominating, before they fan out again in the opposite direction. This is called the *convergence zone*, the point at which managers begin to understand that the approaches to decision making that have served them well are becoming less and less effective.

This pattern becomes even more dramatic when you look at the scores for top-performing managers. (Salary was used as a proxy for success – an imperfect

Leadership styles: Experienced leaders are flexible and integrative

A *Average leadership style scores*

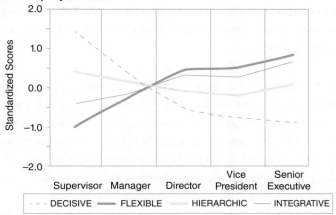

B *Average leadership style scores for highest compensated 20% of executives and managers*

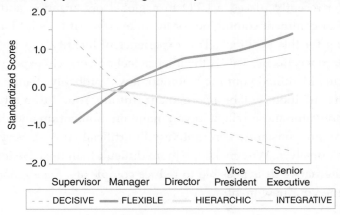

C *Average leadership style scores for lowest compensated 20% of executives and managers*

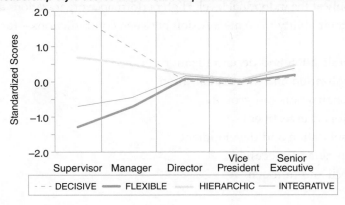

Figure 4 Decision Styles
Source: Brousseau et al (*Harvard Business Review*, February 2006): The Seasoned Executive's Decision-Making Style, based on proprietary research from Korn/Ferry International

measure, but organizations do tend to pay more for better managers.) Once again, we see the crossover with the most successful people reaching this point a bit earlier than average.

This may be an indicator that they are faster to catch on to the need for new behaviors in their new jobs (Figure 4B). The least successful managers – the bottom 20% in terms of income – start out pretty much as the others, but they don't continue to evolve and their leadership styles remain clustered in an "uncertainty zone" (Figure 4C). This is an illustration of the Peter Principle at work: People are promoted up to their level of incompetence!

If you waver between pursuing two different job opportunities, don't ask yourself which one feels best. The first question you must ask yourself is: What drives me? I recently placed a CEO in a global organization and I vividly remember her comment coming out of the interview: "It is as if I have always been training for this position". This experience of lucidity – as if everything falls into place – is magic. This is the intense feeling you will experience when you have truly identified your life ambition. It will probably change over time, but being life ambitious will be a permanent attitude. Your life ambition is your strongest motivator and it will help you maintain momentum and direction in your life. We are constantly confronted with artificial choices. Very often we create them ourselves. Why make life more difficult than it is? History doesn't show the alternative. It is possible to reduce complexity. *Radical Simplification* could become your new mantra.

The potential of being able to think in both/and solutions instead of either/or is huge, not only at the individual level. High performance organizations are characterized by their ability to create a fusion between contradictions – for example:

⊗ Centralization and decentralization
⊗ Globalization and individualization
⊗ Rationalization and growth
⊗ Profit and investment
⊗ Consolidation and development
⊗ Planning and execution
⊗ Hi-tech and hi-touch

Apple, one of the world's most valuable companies, is on the one hand a superbly creative and user-oriented company – and on the other hand an almost military-like organization as far as strategy, design, and execution is concerned. Steve Jobs called Apple the biggest start-up on the planet. It is not a question of more or better, rather a question of more and better.

Family Versus Work

Two of the most common and harmful dichotomies are the perception that you need to choose between being either a career person or a family person, and that your actions are either in your interest or in the interest of the company. I sense an overwhelming need to look at work life and personal life as two sides of the same coin. I can say with absolute certainty that the opposite view – that the two spheres are separate and put different demands upon you – represents a short-sighted and self-destructive strategy. Executives who behave as two different people at home and at the office live on borrowed time. They are doomed to failure, both professionally and personally. You need to be credible in both spheres, because it takes too much of your energy to maintain a façade. You can only perform optimally if you consistently follow your core values both at home and at work.

In his book *Theory U*, Claus Otto Scharmer[7] underlines the need for alignment between the interests of the individual, the group, the organization, and society. In Figure 5 I have added the World.

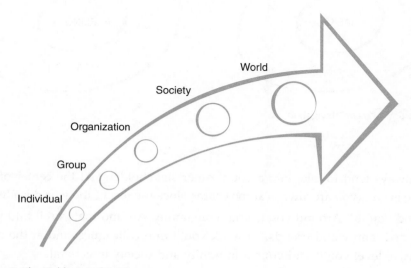

Figure 5 The Noble Art of Scaling

My ambition is to help you create scalability between you as an individual, your group (e.g., your department), your organization (e.g., your firm), your society (e.g., overall trends) and the World (e.g., geopolitics). When you succeed in creating alignment between these dimensions then you reduce friction, and you feel that you are part of something bigger that again is part of something bigger. By reducing the friction between these dimensions you create the basis for a perpetual motion machine. Your Personal Business Plan will allow you to see where the grand project of your life fits into the big picture. Serious PhD research on work–life balance has found that much stress stems not from work but from unrealistic expectations in your private life.[8]

In most work related situations we tend to focus on tasks. Then around those we may have some feelings. In private life it's the other way around. There we focus on feelings and specific tasks have secondary priority. Knowing exactly in which context you are is always beneficial to you. It is only when there is no dichotomy between tasks and feelings that clear solutions emerge. The logic of one context does not necessarily fit the logic of the other context.

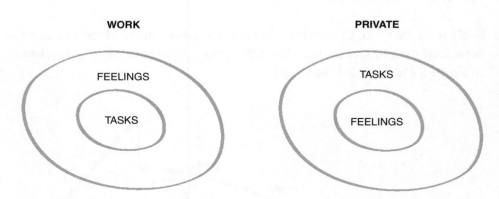

Figure 6 Work/Life Navigation

We always tend to take into account other stakeholders. At the center of the figure is you (you are always at the center, since the rest of the world is always around you ☺). Around you is your core family. Around that you'll find your extended family and friends. At work you'll find colleagues, and at the most inclusive level you'll find your community and society in general.

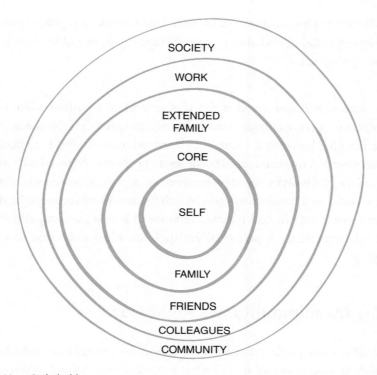

Figure 7 Your Stakeholders

What Baggage from the Past Must I Let Go Of?

In this era of globalization where everyone is competing with more people in more countries and in more ways than ever before, it may well be the question "Why?" that can give us the individual and collective energy needed to compete successfully.

Right now, most leaders have an extremely vivid experience of acute change. It is a brutal digital reality: Change or die! The concept of competition in the future does not entail a battle with traditional and known competitors, but more a battle with ourselves. The door leading to change must be opened from the inside and, for some reason, it always sticks! This constant challenge can be illustrated by using the words of Wayne Gretzky. He was asked how he had become the world's best hockey player. He answered that he had simply listened to his dad. Imagine a kids' team training session. The puck is always in the middle of the biggest clump of players. Dad Gretzky's repeated instruction during hockey training had always been: "Wayne, you've got to skate to where the puck's going to be".[9]

In times with significant mood shifts, it is important to differentiate between fundamental economic changes and mass psychological mechanisms. There is always a time lag between the unrest in financial markets and the effect on the market economy. A financial crisis becomes an economic crisis which turns into a social crisis. It involves the development of a collective expectation, interpreted by some as a breakdown and by others as a breakthrough. In the long run it concerns emotions and the maintenance of long term competitiveness. It is when you experience a perfect storm that you have to be true to your life philosophy.

What is Meaningful to Me Right Now?

One way of avoiding being struck down and out by change is to articulate your personal definition of meaning – so what is meaningful to you? To this end you may also ask yourself: "What preoccupies me?" and "What are my stay-awake issues?"

During our lives we all have the same type of concerns:

- ⊗ We worry about becoming unemployed
- ⊗ We worry about not exercising enough
- ⊗ We worry about the future of our kids
- ⊗ We worry about finding a life partner
- ⊗ We worry about getting an education
- ⊗ We worry about our housing
- ⊗ We worry about the weather
- ⊗ We worry about our health
- ⊗ We worry about the traffic
- ⊗ And so on.

Today, it is important that you define for yourself which of these are relevant limitations for you. You need to clearly state the specific limitations that you are working under in order to be able to disregard all other limitations. You need to get the mental picture of the endless number of opportunities you can create if you are simply aware of the few important stumbling blocks in your way.

Inspiration: The Mysteries of Life

My son, when he was eight, asked me: "Dad, how did you tell mom that you wanted to be her boyfriend?" I told him that first we dated, then we lived together and then we married. It was sort of a revelation to him – you marry your girlfriend – smart! Up till then he had seen couples dating and he had seen married people, but he hadn't made the transitional link between the two.

In Chapter 6 we will deal more in detail with the prerequisites for happiness but for now, I would just like to give you a little insight into the science of happiness.

Inspiration: You Decide 40% of Your Happiness[10]

Your genetic and biological disposition counts for 50% of your happiness[11]. You have a defined happiness set-point that you will return to independently of your life circumstances. Some people are simply happier than others! Only 10% of your happiness is derived from external conditions – that is money, car, house and so on. Just for a minute think about how much time and energy we spend on this disproportionately little share. And now for the good news: The remaining 40% is free for all – you may use it in the best possible way. So you actually have the power to influence 40% of your happiness. That is a really good business proposition. When was the last time you could make a decision where you had the total control of 40% of the outcome? More often than not, our decisions are contingent on lots of external factors and therefore we don't have as much room for maneuvering as we have in this case. Happiness is a direction, not a destination. So you're the boss – you decide!

How Can I Move Forward?

Warren Buffett once said: "It's better to be approximately right than precisely wrong". It's perfectly fine if your way forward is pragmatic; the important thing is that you actually move forward. In the words of Carol Bartz, former CEO of Yahoo: "Fail fast-forward is a favorite motto of mine. It's about not being afraid to fail; and if you do, identify it quickly and move ahead fast so no momentum is lost. I've never been interested in agonizing over what could have or what should have happened. Just get going again".[12] LinkedIn Co-founder and Chairman Reid Hoffman adheres to this view:

> *"* Be diligent about failing fast so that you don't spend five years doing something that's just going to fail. If you're not somewhat embarrassed by your 1.0 product launch, then you've released too late. There's value in launching early, getting engaged with customers, and learning from them. That can direct your progress.[13] *"*

Personal behavior that demonstrates integrity and honesty is primordial for sustained personal success. Most important of all: Only by being in harmony with your inner self is it possible to avoid becoming exhausted in the journey towards success. One of the clearest indicators of malfunction is fatigue. Fatigue is easy to identify when looking at people, and the more you focus the more sensitive you become to the visible signs. People with large black rings under their eyes are very often living a life close to the edge of their performance potential. They may still be able to perform, but the effort of doing so takes a visible toll. This gradual process of exhaustion and burn-out is frequently accompanied by a steady increase in the use of stimulants – taken in order to maintain an illusion of being in control.

Flemming's Tale: From CEO to SDP

Flemming was the CEO of Realdania and the overall theme for his personal reinvention was: **From CEO to SDP** (where SDP stands for Stimulating Dialogue Partner). He was acutely aware that as soon as he passed the CEO relay baton he would only be Flemming, he would no longer be representing billions of dollars in potential grants, sponsorships or investments. So Flemming desperately needed to step up and become a stimulating dialogue partner as an individual. As a result of analyzing his situation, some of his main decisions were to kill some of his habits and break free of weaker people. He would play down relationships with people who drained his energy, which would allow him to focus his energy on his grand project. He also decided to contact his role models and thank them for their support and good example. That would allow him to invent new role models. Flemming also made a firm commitment to contribute with something that only few others would be capable of. You already now discern the contour of a life ambition. He decided to communicate his personal beliefs based on dignity. Regarding the future he made up his mind to treat it as a gigantic firework with lots of colors up in the sky. Flemming wanted to look at the world through a global lens and create value through partnerships and networks. The final picture was still diffuse but at least he sensed a direction.

Jan's Tale: From Thought to Action

Jan had always been a loyal performer. He had done what was needed without asking for recognition or praise. In that sense he was the perfect company man. His personal success criterion had always been solving the issue – regardless of who got the credit. After 15 years working as an auditor and having had three daughters, he felt more in balance than ever. He felt that he had the necessary existential base to again go out looking for adventure in life. His work at CSC provided him with a better integration between family time and work time. Even though he still worked hard, his work was not all-consuming as was the case when he worked as an auditor. Even though he was now part of an organization under significant transformation he wasn't insecure or nervous about the future. He still felt that he had all the possibilities for creating an exciting and challenging future for himself. He had identified the key people who were mission critical for his promotion and was very satisfied with his working relationships and the trust he had built inside the organization. His Annual Appraisal "Consistently Exceeds Expectations" and he was considered to be a driving force for improvement and performing the controller role to a high standard. Through his work with *The Personal Business Plan*, he discovered that he was perhaps too loyal, putting his own interest behind the interest of the team, the interest of the department or the interest of the organization.

Key Learning

- Think of a solution that transcends trade-offs.
- Vision without action is a daydream – action without vision is a nightmare.
- Work at creating a fusion between contradictions – just like high-performance organizations do.
- Perform optimally by consistently following your core values both at home and at work.
- Reduce the friction between the interests of you, the group, the organization, society and the world – then you will have created a perpetual motion machine.
- At work, tasks are surrounded by feelings. At home, feelings are surrounded by tasks.
- Your personal business plan is an answer to all central questions around you.
- Goals are dreams with deadlines.
- The door leading to change must be opened from the inside and, for some reason, it always sticks!
- Avoid being struck down and out by change by articulating your personal definition of meaning.

2

How Can I Thrive?

❝ Life is not a rehearsal ❞
Unknown

One thing has amazed me more than anything else – the simplicity of the recipe for sustainable success, personal as well as professional. And let me give it to you straightaway: The secret behind sustained success is doing more of what you like doing, doing less of what you don't like doing and learning to trust yourself in the process.[14]

It is as simple as that, I am happy to say. I have seen it over and over again. And I know it from myself. However, what's not quite so simple is finding out what you like and don't like. It is also challenging to change your behavior so you start doing what you like and stop doing all the stuff that you don't like doing. And that's what *The Personal Business Plan* is all about and will help you find out.

Together we will define your drivers and motivators, your derailers, and your career stallers and stoppers. We will paint a realistic picture allowing you to play to your strengths and damage control regarding your weaknesses. We are aiming at putting you in the perfect personal balance both between work, family, and home, and professionally between your interests, competencies, and possibilities. That is the state which I call "perfect equilibrium". Through this process, you will also get to align your values, skills, and tasks; your energy will be endless. You will have reduced friction in your system and you will be able to perform effortlessly. In other terms, you will maximize your mojo.

The most important prerequisite though for finding out what you like and don't like doing is that you know yourself intimately and understand how you are and why you behave the way you do. When asked about this nine out of ten people say that they know themselves quite well. But most often this is not quite the truth. I believe that we *would like to know* ourselves better than we actually do. But the fact is that we often know our family, nearest friends and colleagues better than we do ourselves. It's not that we actually lie to ourselves; it's just that we are not always up to date with who we actually are. Our surroundings judge us on what we actually do and how we behave, not on some hidden half-fulfilled intention deep inside our head. The others can't see that you have decided to start exercising; they only judge you on your actual physical shape. We seldom spend very much time looking inward at ourselves, instead we spend most of our life looking outwards at the people closest to us. You probably know that – it's much easier spotting strengths and weaknesses in others that in yourself, right?

It is becoming clear in the research literature that for any meaningful or long-lasting change to occur, development must begin with a solid understanding of yourself. [15] Your self-awareness is at the center of your success. So here's the first step to look at who you truly are. Doing this requires you to explicitly describe *your own* impression of yourself and serenely distill your foundational beliefs.

A Stroll Down Memory Lane

Can you remember your first memory? Think back and try to visualize it. Just reflect – take your time. It may not be easy at first, but then slowly you will start drifting down memory lane. Your first memory may be playing with your siblings at your grandparent's house when you were two years old. Or getting a little brother when you were four years old, or breaking your leg when you were six years old . . . Jot it down on a piece of paper, first the memory and then the year. Then consider which feelings you associate with the specific memory, whether they are positive or negative; for instance, playful, summer, warm.

Take a look at it for as long as you please, and when you are ready, stroll a bit further down memory lane. We are about to do a long list of snapshots and memories of important events from your life. Often it takes a while for the childhood memories to start arriving, but once you get going, they will keep popping up like popcorn in a hot pot. All you have to do is write down whatever comes to mind and the feelings – good or bad – associated to your memories. It may be joy, sadness, guilt, desperation, envy, anything goes. You may have a very vivid and warm memory of painting a fence together with your dad at age nine. Or it might be a memory from fourth grade of a favorite yellow dress, which pops up next. Or the day when you became the winner of a really important soccer match. Then move further along your life. Memories from your adolescence? Your first romance? Graduation? Jot it down in shorthand along with the year. Good as well as bad, big as well as small. You may have a lot of memories, you may have few. Both are equally good. Memories from your years in college? Illness? Parties? Friends? Your first job? Death in the family? Marriage? Your first child? Write it down, whatever comes to mind.

I think you are getting the idea now: What you are writing down is a simple but important biography of *you* and all the major and significant events in your life so far including its peaks and valleys. And you mustn't be afraid of the valleys. We all occasionally have personal crises – it's called living. The important thing is how you handle your life crises and what you learn from them. You may consider them as a hidden experience capital – a personal buffer that you can use in order to deal with your private dilemmas – now and in the future. Seen in this light, your life becomes intriguing, exciting, and purposeful. Most people want the same things but arrive at them differently. You play the main part in the story of your life and you yourself are the storyteller. I bet you have never taken the time to look back at your own life and write down your *entire* story. That's what you are going to do now.

The important thing here is that in order to build your future, you have to document your past and define some of the game changing happenings of your life. If you really know your past and have come to terms with all of your personal history, it will be much easier for you to understand and control your own future. Knowing who you are today will help you not only become the person you want to be tomorrow, but will also make it possible for you to reach your goals no matter how ambitious they are! And don't forget: the more ambitious you are, the more fun you will have when you move towards making your dreams come true.

Let's go back to collecting events from your life – both positive and negative – that have been meaningful to you. We shall put them into a template, and from your long list of events of your life you will make a graphic framework, which I call **Heaven and Hell**: A graph of your life and your wellbeing. It is both a diagnostic and an operational tool, which will allow you to put your ups and downs in life into perspective.

In order to achieve this we'll sort your memories out and rank them according to their relative intensities. The exercise will help you structure your past and present emotions and put them into a high level perspective. You will feel comfortable with your present challenges because you will have the benefit of reflection – the more you reflect the more stress resistant and robust you become.

Exercise: Heaven and Hell

On a piece of paper draw a horizontal line which represents your lifespan. Beginning to the left is the start of your life story – probably beginning with your birth. The horizontal axis represents time in years, and along this line you plot in all the major events of your life. In the vertical axis you plot in your wellbeing at the different events in your life. If it's positive, you plot it in above the horizontal line, if it's negative you plot it in below. So *Heaven* is above the horizontal axis and *Hell* is beneath.

There is one very important thing, you must know before doing this exercise. You have to be as honest and frank assessing yourself as possible – rather too brutal than too soft on yourself. You have to include all the fiascos and difficult episodes from your life as well as all the successes. Otherwise you will be wasting your time. Don't hide anything – the only person you are cheating is you.

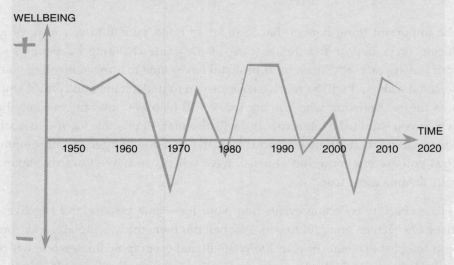

Figure 8 Heaven and Hell

My biggest aim with this exercize is to help you clearly define what success is for you, so you can find out what your future goals are to be. Some periods in your life will be prosperous. This exercise will allow you to prioritize work criteria and personal criteria on the same scale. I see many executives who seem to be handling two separate and independent scales: Overload on the work scale doesn't necessarily have any impact on the personal scale – or rather, they would like to perceive it that way. Of course it is not true. If you are totally stressed out on the job, then your family will suffer. What is true is that you might not notice it, because you're too busy!

Just in order to show you where we're going, in Figure 9 I have plotted an actual case of one of my former clients, whom I shall name John. His life story runs like this:

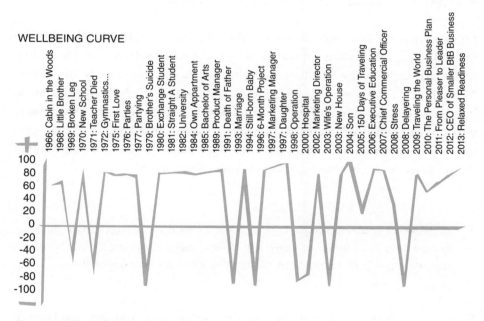

Figure 9 John's Wellbeing Curve

John was a former top level executive at an international fast moving consumer goods company who came to me to get inspiration for his career onwards. I vividly remember my first meeting with John. He was a relaxed and tanned middle-aged man with a certain boardroom appearance. He entered the room and seemed very much in control. I instantly liked him – he seemed fair and solid. He had a wife, two kids, an upward-going career, but had recently been *delayered*. In order to overcome the shock, he had chosen to take some time off and travel the world. But of course he was aware that he needed to get back into the saddle. That was why he had come to me.

I asked him to fill me into the details of his life and he told me the following story. He had had a peaceful childhood and remembered with joy the day his little brother was born. One of his sadder memories was breaking a leg and not being able to play with his friends. His father got a new job and they moved to a new city where he started in a new school. There was an excellent teacher, who did a lot to integrate John in the new class. The first day at school there was a banner with "Welcome John" in the class! John felt great and was devastated when the teacher was killed in a car crash. That was his first encounter with death – *childhood is the kingdom where nobody dies.*[16]

I quietly noticed that when he started describing his life, it was a bit difficult for him to express feelings. It was as if he had limited self-insight. He seldom described the reasoning behind his behavior, more often simply the action: "And then I . . ." There is the question of pride – it takes a little time for me to build trust and get behind the façade that has been carefully crafted over many years. My experience is that the dilemmas or issues that are brought forward in the first sessions very seldom remain as the crucial or vital few at the end of the sessions. In the beginning, form prevails over content.

> At thepersonalbusinessplan.com you will find a digital *Wellbeing Analysis Tool* that will help you with your Heaven and Hell exercise and plotting the wellbeing curve described in this chapter. You will also find John's full story for inspiration.

Now it is your turn to follow the same procedure and complete the Heaven and Hell exercise yourself. As you do so, you will see your life unfold before your eyes. You will probably discover great pleasure in being allowed to tell your story without interruption. We are all able to recollect significant turning points from our life, but we very seldom get the opportunity to tell the whole story. The relaxed readiness of the moment enables creativity and new memories come up by association. It takes a couple of hours to go through the exercise, and at the end it is possible to connect the dots chronologically. This means that we obtain a sort of rollercoaster picture where you may end up having more events above the line or having more events below the line.

However, most of the leaders with whom I have gone through this process are surprised to see how much of their life has actually taken place above the line. So it is a powerful visual representation of how much you have to be thankful for.

After you have plotted the first couple of events you will be able to calibrate the instrument so that the relative positive or negative representation fits your overall impression and recall. Some memories will be personal and some will be professional – taken together they paint a valid picture of your life. Interestingly, you will start comparing personal and professional life events on the same scale. There is great learning to be found in ranking events such as graduation, marriage, birth of a child, illness of a parent, promotion at work, difficulties in school for a child, unemployment, and completing a marathon on a wellbeing scale. What comes out is what you attach importance to – your life anchors. You will see patterns develop. Later on in the book, I will help you take the best from the past and refine this in order to use it selectively, in the right context, in the future.

The picture also clearly shows how quickly things may change – big things, life decisions. Death or derailment may strike overnight. You will probably acknowledge that you have been stunningly fast to adapt to a new situation and rebound after a crisis. Of course, some of the incidents, like the loss of a job or the death of a spouse, are more difficult to handle than others. Even so, if you are able to convince yourself of the bigger positive picture, surviving these traumatic events will be easier and you will be better equipped for the next challenges in your life.

It's important that you allow yourself plenty of time to work with your curve and reflect about your past life. Get in touch with your inner workings and be totally honest with yourself – let your ambitions and dreams become obvious. Apart from drawing your wellbeing curve, you must at the same time write down in your own personal business plan the findings, inspirations, and thoughts that come across, because the simple action of writing them down creates a commitment to the implementation.

You will know that you are finished with the exercise when you look at it and get that feeling of clarity, when you look at it and read it all over again with a sort of WOW! feeling. *Is it this simple? I can do this!* You may have to go back to your own wellbeing curve a couple of times before you are perfectly happy with it.

It's important that you do not move on further in this chapter until you are actually happy with your wellbeing curve. It will serve as your basic reference point for the rest of Your Personal Business Plan and for all the other exercises which you are to do throughout this book.

Inspiration: Could I Have a Cat Then?

Here's a story concerning a local CEO of a global advertising agency, who had come to me to get a new perspective on his professional career.

Eric was a highly energetic, self-assured man in his mid-forties with a very solid appearance. I started coaching him, and soon asked him to do the Heaven and Hell exercise. Working through his life graph, we got to a point a couple of years earlier in his life story, where he had collapsed at work due to stress. It was a life and death situation but although Eric plotted this in as one of his low points, he explained how he had gotten over it by changing his diet and started working out frequently. But as I heard Eric tell his story, I could sense that personally, he wasn't in balance and so asked him how his family had reacted to his stroke. Eric recalled how his four year old daughter had visited him in the hospital. When he told her that maybe he was going to die, her spontaneous response was to ask: "Could I have a cat then?" Eric was allergic to pets and for many years had denied her a cat. His daughter's almost too honest lack of interest in his wellbeing had hurt him deeply.

Now, looking back at the incident and having time to reflect about her reaction, Eric understood it in a much larger perspective. And plotting it in his life graph, he judged it as worse than the stroke itself. For the first time he truly, deeply realized that he had prioritized his work over his family for a very long period and wasn't in sound balance. Eric realized that not only could he compare incidents of his professional life with events in his personal life, but also that if he wanted a balanced life with a sound relationship with his daughter, he would have to take a new look at his entire life. This insight became the point of departure for Eric's further development. He worked tirelessly with his equilibrium and within two years he had both reduced his working week by a quarter, and mended his relationship with his daughter.

What Do I Like Doing?

> ❝ We don't stop playing because we get old.
> We get old because we stop playing. ❞
> *Sir George Bernard Shaw*

The ability to opt out of the rat race will eventually become one of the key factors of obtaining "the good life". The new polarization in society is not primarily found between those who have an education and those who don't. Instead it is found between those who actively exploit and control their freedom, and those who choose to see themselves as being victims. It seems that more and more people are able to grasp this and that there is status attached to demonstrating control. We want to signal that we have control of our lives. We need to think creatively and act decisively. Your challenge now is to learn to live from what you like doing. We have always talked about the importance of navigating and choosing; but in the future it will be important to keep hold of the priorities that are meaningful to you in your life. The rest needs to be screened off because we are approaching a point of saturation – there is a definite need for radical simplification.

I have talked to many leaders who feel stretched – sometimes near to breaking point. Some of the most successful in terms of wealth have many activities across different functions, roles and geographies. One particular executive springs to mind. He represents a private equity company; he is on the board of several listed companies and he has minority interests in several companies in the US, Europe, and China. His extended family is dispersed and he has small children. The challenge for him is to rediscover his roots, and to find continuity and meaning in the sum of his activities. When you are an expert, it is always easy to take on new responsibilities and help other people out, whereas "No" would sometimes be the most appropriate answer when you are trying to maintain your own priorities.

Ironically, some of the hardest-working people I know are self-employed and do not have any financial reason to work. But they still want to show their father, their spouse or the world what they can accomplish. You are your own harshest employer. This reminds me of the paradox described by Joseph Heller in *Catch-22*:

> *"* If a fighter pilot is willing to risk his life in air raids then he must be mad. And if he is mad he has the right to apply for exemption from the raids. But if he is able to apply for exemption, then he shows that he is normal. Hence his application must be refused, and he does not escape flying air raids.[17] *"*

> *"* Yesterday is history. Tomorrow is a mystery.
> Today is a gift. That's why it is called the present. *"*
> *Eleanor Roosevelt*

Time is the only democratically allocated resource – we all have the same amount of time at our disposal each day. The question is how we choose to use it. You may be tempted to excuse yourself by saying that you do not have time to reinvent yourself. The fact is that we work only approximately 60% of our time. If you count evenings, weekends, public holidays and holidays you have lots of time. Over a lifetime most people spend more time in front of the television than at work! And yes – it's okay to check the calculation.

Most of us have a tendency to procrastinate. In fact, if it were not for the last minute, nothing would be done. But how we use our time – or how we waste it – is always a matter of personal choice. Successful entrepreneurs become successful by using creativity on the fly to deal with challenges, they do not spend time predicting the future – instead they act constantly in a dynamic way – finetuning their efforts. Although we may define it differently, we all aspire to status.

In our hyperactive, present day business culture, time is the new status symbol. The CEO of a large bank once confided: "I never use my driver during the day. I never take taxis from one part of the city to attend a meeting in another. I walk. That's how I demonstrate that I control my own schedule and how I choose to use my time!"

So, what do you like doing?

Forced Writing Exercise: Likes

Take 6½ minutes to write down what you like doing. You must write without interruption. Associations will follow freely. If nothing else, then write your shopping list. Don't stop writing. You can always delete. Don't worry. You can do it. Now!

You may like to use the template at the end of the book and at thepersonalbusinessplan.com for this exercise.

What Don't I Like Doing?

In order to optimize your energy, it is not enough to do what you like doing. It is also necessary to stop doing what you do *not* like doing[18]

We all have tasks or duties that we actually dislike doing but we seldom focus exclusively on this dark side. My experience is that this feeling of limitation and resistance is very often linked to specific situations and to individuals who make them insecure. Some people have this effect on you and often it is because they mirror you in a way that you do not necessarily appreciate. So just think about what would happen if you could simply eliminate the situations or people that suck energy out of you. I am perfectly aware that we have moral obligations and that politeness dictates us to behave according to the accepted cultural norms, but nonetheless – wouldn't it be great?

I would recommend taking the necessary conflicts head on by stating your views clearly. Make the issue explicit and address it without any more beating around the bush. Find out what makes you tense, and do something about it. Aristotle said that nature abhors a vacuum – translated into leadership terms this means that if you choose not to occupy a space others will. If this entails the deterioration or limitation of your sphere of influence, then your career and private life will suffer from your indecision or lack of courage. And you will live an incomplete life.

Forced Writing Exercise: Dislikes

Identify what derails you and what your "show stoppers" are. Which specific factors tend to destabilize you? Is there a pattern? If you think through the situations that did not work out very well for you, what were the common elements that drained you of energy?

Once again take 6½ minutes. Be honest with yourself and write down your show stoppers. Don't stop writing and follow all your associations. Don't worry. You can do it. Again!

You may like to use the template at the end of the book and at thepersonalbusinessplan.com for this exercise.

The fundamental problems in life concern "getting along" and "getting ahead" – developing relationships and developing a career. These themes exist in a state of tension that is resolved in social interaction. Some people are better than others at resolving this tension and finding solutions to this problem; they tend to move into leadership positions. Rigidity, poor relationships, and the inability to lead teams are, according to a Center for Creative Leadership study, the most common traits of executives who derail.[19] Managers who derail often have high levels of expertise but many are arrogant and have a disdain for teamwork. Leadership is a contact sport. The blind spot of leadership is self-awareness.

In order to enhance your self-awareness, you have to take a deep dive and confront the barriers and burdens you feel when pressured in your role as leader. As in most important situations you already know the answer; you simply have to verbalize it. I have experienced many leadership development sessions, where a person is placed in the "hot seat" and asked to present a personal dilemma. He or she is then asked questions by the other participants. As the session develops it very often becomes clear *to the audience* what the obvious choice of action is. The answers all tend to point in that direction. However, and interestingly enough, the interviewee does not realize it yet. It is as if his or her body already knows the answer, but the answer has not yet been verbalized and hence has not earned its rational legitimacy. The condition could be expressed like this: "I have made my decision, but I do not know it yet".

Similar situations can be experienced when you use reflective teams. When you, as the central person, hear others talking about you and discussing your issues it clarifies your mind. The nature of your objections (which you are not allowed to communicate) hints at the fundamental issues, the core conflict. One of the world's most influential investors, George Soros has recounted that he learned to recognize that a backache signaled time to sell, even before he was consciously aware he had made a bad investment.[20] Thus my recommendation is to release the energy bound in your old tensions by confronting them. Break the mold and enter the fray. By doing this you will reduce your tension – both mentally and physically.

Inspiration: Feedback Perspective

In order to collect supplementary input about yourself, try asking a couple of colleagues, friends and possibly your boss and/or spouse the following questions:

- If you were describing me to a very good friend, what would be the first words that come to mind?
- What do you think I'm really good at?
- What do you see as my driving force? In other words what do you think truly motivates me?
- What are three things that make me effective, and that you feel I should continue to display?
- What are three things that could make me more effective, and that you feel I should display more?
- What are three things that are making me ineffective, and that you feel I should stop doing, or at least do less of?
- What else differentiates me from the rest?

These questions are given to potential participants as preparation for the INSEAD Advanced Management Program.[21]

How Can I Learn to Trust My Intuition?

Excellent ideas should be seen as lighthouses that clearly indicate the direction to be taken. As a leader you must trust your intuition as this is the sum of your experience. A solid self-understanding and insight is fundamental if you are to act quickly and decisively. The condition for optimal decision making is to listen to subtle signals and then through analysis and reflection to create a synthesis. In order to split the problem or issue into its constituent parts and then to recreate these into a whole you, as a leader, must have free and available mental capacity that allows you to focus on the central questions – the *Vital Few*.

The work with the Vital Few is a central task for any ambitious leader. The best opportunity to convert your dreams into realistic goals and concrete deadlines lies in the clarification of these questions. The more times, you think the thought, the more real it becomes – the rest, then, is a question of discipline. But, right now, when you are burying yourself in activity, rule number one is: Stop digging!

Anne M. Mulcahy, Chairman and former CEO for Xerox Corporation once said that Xerox had run out of crises and that she considered that a problem.[22] As the external acute pressure on a company disappears it becomes more difficult to initiate great changes, including that of totally revising the fundamental business model. Therefore, it becomes imperative to create an internal pressure. Only when we have acknowledged what we stand for as a person or an organization, and what we want to stand for in the future, it will be possible for us to communicate this convincingly to our stakeholders. The reflection and the process behind this self-understanding is a good investment of time and energy. A good night's sleep and peace of mind cannot be bought at too high a price. Often the best recipe for sleep is the good results of the day.

When leaders with deeply rooted opinions and standpoints have the opportunity to implement effective actions, we can achieve a collective lift in the organization's ability to generate brilliant results. In fact, in order to crystallize ambitious goals we are forced to focus on our talents. Often the margin between success and fiasco is tiny. So you have to make it happen – just do it. You project what you think you are and believe yourself to be; winning is seeing yourself in control, and thus, being in control. When you reflect deeply, you realize that there are many versions of reality and hence many truths. John Stuart Mill expresses this in the following way: "He who knows only his own side of the case knows little of that".[23] So humility, curiosity and active listening play a major role in personal success. Sometimes the best questions are the obvious ones – the ones that nobody asks due to some misunderstood sense of politeness. The Greek historian and author Thucydides (about 460–395 BC) recommended doing the best you can do in your own area of control – the rest will follow. You are only able to respond within your own sphere of influence. Simply look at the origin of the word responsibility – *response ability!* You need to apply aggressive and forceful leverage to that which you can control; define your own agenda – not that of others.

If top management is able to talk honestly about its values in a way that appeals to the target (customer) group, then the values (and hence the organization) will be perceived as attractive. Emotions are the real thing. This fits perfectly with the concept of the triple bottom line where the corporation must satisfy demands from shareholders, society and employees. Demands for integrity and corporate social responsibility have become mandatory. The corporation must create real value for the customer and not only perceived value for the stock market.

Ingvar Kamprad, the founder of IKEA, tends to ask collaborators about the meaning of their job, that is, their *raison d'être*. The real question behind the question is: What is your significance to me as a customer? Only when we can adequately answer this question, we will be able to see our solutions and services in a real customer perspective. If you want to move a mountain, start with the small rocks.

Flemming's Tale: How Can I Thrive?

And what did our hero, Flemming get out of the Wellbeing Analysis presented in this chapter? Actually, many inspirational findings: He discovered that he was energized by complexity and challenge. He also expressed that he enjoyed analyzing and structuring new themes – and meeting new people! One thing that Flemming feared was wasting 10 years of his life. He decided on a new rule of living: Shit happens – forget it fast! He also decided working on a new version of himself: First convincing himself before convincing others. His aim was to become ambitious enough to surprise both himself and others. In some way it's better to burn up than to fade away. He would listen to criticism and act accordingly instead of playing it down. And then he would identify a personal target that would be capable of overshadowing his past position in Realdania. He needed to substitute his past performance with a greater goal.

Jan's Tale: How Can I Thrive?

Jan's findings went in another direction. He focused primarily on improving the quality of his daily life and carrying out some of his "forgotten dreams". In the short term, this meant planning and prioritizing experiences with his family, that is, short weekend trips, holidays, and a sabbatical. More long term, it meant revitalizing dreams about a farm with horses, a sailing boat, deep ocean diving and track days with Porsche. Jan actually ended up buying a sailing boat (an X-99) before the end of our sessions, showing how powerful the work of the subconscious is. What you focus on, you get! Jan also consciously focused on doing good and spreading happiness by small actions such as bringing back flowers for his wife. He would prioritize teamwork, talent development, and immersion in exciting professional subjects, history and biographies. He also realized that he disliked working with people he didn't respect and being amongst a group of people he didn't know. All in all company politics and being the center of a social activity seemed unattractive to Jan.

Key Learning

- Face your personal crises – it's called living.
- Play the main part in the history of your life and be the storyteller.
- Do more of what you like doing, do less of what you don't like doing and learn to trust yourself in the process.
- Accept that you are judged on what you actually do and how you behave, not on your intentions.
- Connect who you were with who you are now with the one you are to become.
- Be responsible for your own happiness; reinvent yourself and live your new and improved version.
- Document your life and prepare your future.
- Your blind spot is self-awareness.
- As a leader you must trust your intuition as this is the sum of your experience.
- When you are burying yourself in activity, rule number one is: Stop digging!

3

When Do I Perform at My Best?

// Goals are dreams with deadlines //
Diana Scharf Hunt

We are progressing towards formulating your life ambition, the most valuable element in Your Personal Business Plan and the compass on your journey towards lifelong development and success. Your life ambition is the sum of what gives you meaning. What do you want to be known for?

Before we get that far I'm going to help you work out what has driven you in your career up till now. Our aim is to document the conditions under which you have thrived. Each and every time I have worked together with executives on the following exercise it has resulted in "eyes-wide-open" and *wow!* reactions. When you have completed it you will, for the first time ever, be able to *in a completely precise manner* describe why you were happier in your second job than in your first or vice versa.

Step 1

The diagram is quite simple. First you fill out the top row with your jobs up till now (including years). You can find an empty diagram at the back of the book and also at thepersonalbusinessplan.com.

I want to make it absolutely clear that you need to start with a blank left column. The following list can be used as inspiration, but it is your life and there is no One Size Fits All – we are all a sample of one ☺.

Step 2

Now think back to your first job. Note in the left column which factors made you feel good at the time. Possible answers about your first job could

Table 1 The Functional Conditions

Functional Conditions	First job 19ab–19cd	Second job 19cd–19ef	Third job 19ef–19gh	Fourth job 19gh–20ij	Fifth job 20ij–20kl	Present job 20kl–Now
Challenges						
Responsibility						
Trust						
Projects						
Salary						
Team						
Learning						
Adventure						
Recognition						
Travel						
Processes						
Business Model						
Leadership						
P&L Responsibility						
People Management						
Value Chains						
Energy						
Strategy						
Coaching						
Mergers and Acquisitions						
Entrepreneurship						
Corporate Social Responsibility						
Communication						
Integrity						
Role Model						
Status						

be challenges, responsibility, trust, projects, salary, team, or other characteristics. Fill in the appropriate characteristics in the first column of the table.

Step 3

Take your next job and carry out the same exercise. Since this position probably represents a promotion, you will probably be able to add to the list. Possible additional answers could be learning, adventure, recognition, travel, processes, a business model or other alternatives which are relevant to you. Now, look at your third job and add what comes to mind.

Possible answers could be leadership, P&L responsibility, people management, value chains and so on.

Step 4

When you have finished going through all your jobs – and this could be 10 different positions or more – use Table 2 to rate each of your positions for each of the characteristics. 1 = Positive, 2 = Neutral and 3 = Negative. Think of it as awarding them a Gold (1), Silver (2) or Bronze (3) medal. Start by going through all the characteristics for your first job. Then continue with your second job, and so on.

Table 2 The Rating of the Functional Conditions

Functional Conditions	First job 19ab–19cd	Second job 19cd–19ef	Third job 19ef–19gh	Fourth job 19gh–20ij	Fifth job 20ij–20kl	Present job 20kl–Now
Challenges	1	1	1	1	1	1
Responsibility	1	2	1	1	1	1
Trust	1	2	3	1	1	1
Projects	1	3	2	1	2	1
Compensation	1	2	2	1	1	1
Team	1	2	2	1	1	2
Learning	2	1	2	1	2	3
Adventure	3	1	3	1	2	3
Recognition	3	1	3	1	2	1
Travel	3	1	2	2	2	2
Processes	3	1	2	2	2	2
Business Model	3	1	2	1	1	1
Leadership	3	2	1	1	1	1
P&L Responsibility	3	3	1	1	1	1
People Management	3	3	1	1	1	1
Value Chains	3	3	1	1	1	1
Energy	2	2	2	1	2	3
Strategy	3	3	2	1	1	1
Coaching	3	3	2	1	1	1
Mergers and Acquisitions	3	3	3	1	1	1
Entrepreneurship	3	3	3	3	1	1
Corporate Social Responsibility	3	3	3	3	1	2
Communication	3	3	3	3	1	1
Integrity	1	2	2	2	2	1
Status	3	3	3	2	2	1
Role Model	3	3	3	2	2	1

As you work through Table 2, you will start to see a pattern emerge. Some of the positions in which you thrived share some of the same characteristics. There will probably be some rows where you have many scores of "1" for most of your recent jobs. This indicates a fundamental decision criterion for you. In this example it could be challenges, responsibility, leadership, P&L responsibility, people management, and value chains. You will soon be able to identify the criteria that are critical for your success and your happiness. You can also analyze your present job and note where there is not a perfect fit; you may already have a feeling about this without actually having been able to specify the details – but now, it's a different story!

Step 5

Just for fun you may want to add up your scores for each position and see what your best job until now has been – remember, the lower the score the better the position. Keep in mind that these criteria are not weighted. If the results truly represent your own impression, then it validates the tool; if not, some important parameters are missing. When you consider your present job, is there one of the important decision criteria that is not met?

Step 6

Having looked backwards over your career, you can now turn towards the future. What functional conditions should be met in your ideal job? Are there dimensions that you have not yet challenged but that you would love to have a go at? Could it be the job title? Perhaps working for a blue-chip company? Maybe you would like to strive for more independence at work? Try working with different dimensions in order to create an accurate representation of your ideal job situation.

Step 7

Now try to put in your ideal job profile in Table 2 and see how it looks. From now on you will be able to put every new job opportunity you create into this grid and this will allow you to evaluate it objectively – taking your career history into account. We all have a tendency to crave for what we don't have. So, if you work in a local organization, you might prefer to work in a global organization; if you work in a small organization, you might dream about a large organization etc. But, looking back over your career, how did you feel when you were actually in that situation?

Every job has its advantages and disadvantages and you risk being colored by two general mechanisms in human psychology. First you tend to romanticize aspects from the past. Second you tend to believe that the grass is greener on the other side of the fence. The dynamics of human behavior haven't changed. This functional condition framework will help you think back and eliminate the wishful thinking. When you have experienced different types of organizations, you will know which type of culture suits you best. This recognition will enable you to produce the best results while thriving in the process.

Step 8

In Table 2 I have put some of the 1's in green. These represent the positive dimensions that are added by a job change. When you fill out your own diagram, you will notice the same pattern. Change gives new opportunities – you simply see the world in a new perspective – and that energizes you. Now it's possible for you to put your ideal job in the last column – you are now aware of your trigger dimensions and can therefore easily put in the fundamental functional conditions that are necessary for you to thrive. In the future you will be able to put any conceivable job opportunity into the matrix and evaluate it objectively up against your ideal job specification and your career history. It will allow you to make more well-informed decisions – and approach your life ambition in a confident manner.

All along you had the knowledge needed to make informed decisions – you simply needed to surface it. You can use the tool for one more thing – namely to find out when you run the risk of compromising. Have another look at your matrix and try to pinpoint when you ended up doing something which didn't comply with whom you wanted to be, professionally or personally. At the time you probably simply played a game with yourself, thinking that "it couldn't be different" or that you "didn't have the choice". If you want to defend your personal integrity, which in the long run is necessary for a happy life, it is valuable to remind yourself that you again may end in a situation where you need to manifest your limits. Then you will be able to explicitly formulate why you don't want to repeat the mistakes from the past.

What Does Success Look Like to Me?

Imagine being in the state of mind which follows your picture of success. Personally I know precisely what I see when I close my eyes. There is a group of people on the world scene who together make up the so-called "Global Lecture Circuit". They are less than 200 and when they are sent for they fly to another continent and make keynote speeches. They are perceived as so knowledgeable and valuable that they have obtained near total freedom in their life, both personally, professionally, and financially. At the same time, they do something they love and which represents an inner meaning to them.

To me such a life is the ultimate picture of success, at least combined with a rich family life.

There may be many reasons that you will never experience your picture of success. Even though you succeed in collecting all the necessary competencies, it takes a lot of luck to win the Nobel Prize or become a billionaire. Nonetheless you will experience it as valuable to document your dreams in writing. They are much better pointers than, for example, your environment's expectations of you. They give you a feeling of purpose.

Please find below a series of good advice when defining your picture of success.

Purpose is the Invisible Leader

Make the greatest possible impact over the longest period of time. Sustained success is about who you are and not what you have. Winston Churchill stated that success is going from failure to failure with no loss of enthusiasm. Tough times never last, but tough people do. Believe in what you are doing. Success in a career, including financial success, demands that you fully invest yourself. If you don't, you will be at a serious disadvantage compared with those who *do* believe in what they are doing. Most managers are corporate people protecting their own mortgages. Given that people are inherently selfish, gigantic bonuses and exit packages are understandable. For the individual it is a question of securing his or her future genealogy. Most of us want the same thing: We want our children to succeed.

Start Early

Choose the right boss – choose one who can become your role model and mentor. Be aware of how your choices and goals support your career – it is important that both you and others can see that your career is progressive; if you are in doubt, consult professionals. Remember the Blue Chip Effect; when high quality brands are on your CV, the readers unconsciously let the emotional part of their brain, the limbic system, act. When a reader, for example, sees The Coca-Cola Company or Apple on a CV, positive connotations tend to arise. Afterwards, the rational argument is: "If the candidate is good enough for them, then the candidate is good enough for me".

Take Risks

Every person must venture into unknown territory. However, we don't all need to follow the example of the daredevil Felix Baumgartner who, in 2012, did his space skydive. "What the mind of man can conceive and believe, it can achieve."[24] Remember that the influence of any decision equals the product of the quality of the decision and the acceptance of the decision. Your goal is to be the best – forget about the rest. Don't be afraid if progress seems a little slow; you shouldn't be afraid of going slowly, only of standing still. When I started in Executive Search more than 17 years ago, I asked the president of the corporation how long it took before clients started calling rather than the other way around. His answer was "Well, the first 10 years are the hardest!"

How Do You Feel When You Are Already There?

When you want to conduct a major change in your career, imagine what success tastes like. Success is to wake up with a smile on your face. Success is balance and equilibrium. The challenge is to create continuity in change. Here, we need to discern between change and transition. Change is external, situational, and can occur quickly. In contrast, transition is internal, psychological, and always takes longer. If change corresponds to the decision, then transition corresponds to the implementation. The question then, is not only about achieving success, but also about managing success properly when you get it.

Prepare Yourself Mentally in Advance

People tend to work at one level below where they are now, but to be successful you need to work where you *are*, not where you *were*. Perhaps the biggest pitfall you face is assuming that what has made you successful so far in your career will continue to do so. You need to accelerate your integration into the new role by "unlearning" your old tried and trusted ways as fast as possible. This means preparing yourself mentally to move into your new role by letting go of your old job and embracing the new one. By doing this you can be sure that you will hit the ground running. Relearning to learn can be painful, however, and the process of transition into a new job may revive some deep fears about your capabilities that you thought you had long laid to rest. When this doubt hits you, you may seek comfort in the thought that the least developmental job is your boss's job. So when it hurts, it is actually because you are learning big time and becoming a better version of yourself!

Act as if You Were Already at the Next Level of Your Career

You must make yourself a player in the organization by not only focusing on short-term results but also on long-term relationships. Make your own role visible and create understanding of the value you personally add to the corporation. Ensure that your success criteria lie in direct continuation of the corporation's business model. Actually, I prefer the words *business logic* – following a single business model is risky – the companies that succeed are nimble and ever-changing.

Develop the Business as a Whole

Many of the executives who are today functional directors spend a lot of time optimizing operations in their own department instead of developing the business as a whole. So they concentrate their forces on their own silo. A marketing director will typically focus on the optimal use of, for instance, the media budget, a HR director may focus on optimizing the budget for education and a production director often concentrates on automation of production. But these efforts hardly arouse interest or generate respect outside the respective departments involved. The risk, therefore, is to gamble on delivering results that are less visible for others in the organization, what I call doing invisible work.

Always Keep Top Management Perspective

For you personally, this silo-focus means that you do not put yourself in a position to handle a high profile job – on the contrary, it represents more of a self-limitation. A career is built upon qualifying yourself for the next higher position and how can you do that if, in your work activities, you maintain the silo perspective? As an Executive Search Consultant I often see functional directors putting emphasis on specific professional success criteria that, in reality, do not have any great influence on the collective development of the corporation. Real value – both for you and for the corporation – is created by contributing with new holistic initiatives. I am tempted to say that the perspective should always be that of top management. So, ask yourself: Which of my leadership initiatives create growth and progress for the corporation as a whole?

Identify Your Pet Project

You are probably familiar with the situation where a colleague in the management team puts a well-documented report on the table. Your first thought is: How did he or she get the time to write this? The probable outcome is that the executive in question receives more resources in the form of people or funding, while you simply continue to carry out your operational tasks in your department. Real value is created through initiatives which would not have been undertaken if a person had not prioritized a task that was above the department perspective and that contributed directly to the bottom line.

Get P&L Responsibility

From a career perspective you must always work on tasks that are on the agenda of top management. It is important to get experience from different functions in the corporation. If you work with marketing, be sure to get hands-on sales experience. If you work in a staff function, be sure to get real life experience from a line responsibility. Under all circumstances be sure to get P&L responsibility. No matter what, you should launch yourself into projects that have a business signal value and that contribute to the image of you as someone who looks at the corporation from a top management perspective.

> *" The road to success is always under construction. "*
> *Lily Tomlin*

Celebrate Your Victories

Sometimes we run companies as if we were participants in a marathon race without a finish line. We are busy with business, busy living, busy dying. And why are we so busy? It might be because we want to keep the meaninglessness of our existence at bay. For many people, work is an attempt to avoid absurdity and to forget the loneliness of our life. When we listen to it, the silence can be frightening. We need to bring back the breaks. We must set a finish line. And we need to have a harvest festival from time to time. Celebrate your victories; success rituals are fundamental to sustained performance. At the end of the day, the greatest failure is to be successful and not satisfied.

If Your Company Was a Person, Would It Be Your Friend?

Jeffrey Immelt, the President and CEO of GE once said: "People don't come to work to be number one or number two in a specific market or to achieve a return on investment of twenty percent. They want bigger goals. They want to find a meaning in life".[25] The corporation needs to make itself available as an attractive identity-creating and culture-carrying community. The attraction and retention of talent is not a task one function in the corporation can fulfill all alone. There needs to be alignment between the messages from top management and the respective messages from the HR, marketing and communication departments. The role of top management is to orchestrate the effort so that the task is carried out effectively and the corporation's future is secured from a talent perspective. In the end the objective of communication is to reduce uncertainty. There may be many voices, but there should only be one message. Define, describe, deliver.

Success Takes Creativity, Genius and Luck

Success does not come by itself. Claus Otto Scharmer notes that there are two questions at the root of *creativity*: Who is my Self? What is my Work?[26] Self with a capital "S" is your best future possibility. Work with a capital "W" is your purpose, what you are here on Earth to do. Thomas Edison wrote that *genius* consists of 1% inspiration and 99% perspiration. Regarding *luck*, Thomas Jefferson concluded: "I am a great believer in luck and I find the harder I work the more I have of it".

What is My Deep Down Motivation?

All motivation stems from two fundamental drivers. We seek pleasure and we seek meaning. Good food, good company, or sex gives us pleasure and we are very motivated to achieve pleasure. At the time of experiencing it, we feel satis-fied. Unfortunately this feeling does not last and we become hungry, lonely or sexually under-stimulated once more. One can say that the motivation to seek pleasure is, to a certain extent, driven by the wish for the absence of discomfort or pain. As the Dalai Lama points out, life is like a cup of tea – most people drink it without enjoying it.

Before carrying on I would recommend that you think through the motives behind the choices you have made in your life until now. Understanding your own motivation has another advantage: It will help you evaluate the motives of others. This in turn will help you deal with the world in an eye-to-eye manner, where you to a higher degree are capable of anticipating the reaction of others. You can start with questions like: Why do I do what I do? Why do I have the friends I have? What do I seek to achieve and why? Why do I hide information from somebody? Why do I always make the same mistake? Why do I take the chances that I do? And why am I good at this? The more you are aware of your deeper intentions, the more able you will be to act in accordance with them.

You may continue this self-investigation with fundamental questions such as: What would make me happy? What keeps me from achieving this? When do I feel at my best? When do I find my work most fun? What do I dislike about my job? What have I ever developed a passionate interest in? What would make a difference in my perceived quality of life? What do I want to change in the world? What would it mean for me to live in total integrity? What difference would I like to have made, when I look back on my life? What kind of value would I like to have created? What contribution would I be proud of having made? Very often you do not have to look into the world to find the answers to these questions. The inner voice, which is often drowned by the many dos of the day, knows more about our life than most experts.

You will experience being energized by being transparent. Your authenticity will make you reduce the friction created by hunting the perfection of the per-sonal narrative which you know deep down is deceitful. The art is to be able to write about your shame without being ashamed. When you are able to look yourself in the eye and write down what you see, you have come a long way. I have never met a person who didn't seek recognition in one form or another. Many times I've sat with people who describe precisely what type of recognition they are seeking from whom, and as they speak the words it is as if an inner tension leaves their body. Specifically, I recall a CEO who told me that for decades he had been driven by the hope of winning his father's recognition. Figuratively he said "Dad, look at me!" – even long after his dad had died.

I often meet leaders who express a feeling of stress in their lives and a feeling of lack of overview. They have difficulties in transforming information overflow into personal knowledge. Learning transforms information to knowledge and, therefore, it is important to focus on lifelong learning. We all have a need to gain new knowledge so we can continue to be interesting dialogue partners for our stakeholders. Many leaders, therefore, enjoy rituals where at least once a day they look inwards and listen to the messages from their intuitive self. The intellectual process focuses on the answer. Meditation is an immersion which focuses on the question. By meditating you look through yourself. Meditation is dealing honestly with yourself and dialogue is dealing honestly with others. By focusing on your deep down motivation you will be able to reach a breakthrough where you are no longer ashamed of your inner motivation – you have made it explicit both to yourself and to the world – and therefore you may now relax.

Inspiration: Relaxation Perspective

A way of increasing your robustness is to sharpen your body and your mind, so they can function in an integrated way. Breathing exercises help you to remain calm during the stressful moments of the day. The ability to maintain calm and deep breathing are essential in today's leadership. Andrew Weil, MD states that breath control is the most powerful method he has found to reduce anxiety.[27] Being in good physical shape is an important basis for the psychological stamina that you need. The effort of keeping in shape does not drain your energy. On the contrary, there is ample proof that physical exercise creates mental and physical energy.

Here are two free methods: (1) *Breathe in as deeply as you can*, preferably through the nose, deep down into your stomach. The deeper, you breathe, the calmer you become, and the better you are able to keep your lucidity and overview even in the most hectic situations. (2) *Be in the now*. It sounds banal, but one of the most important causes of stress is not what is actually happening but the ideas we are generating about what is happening. Trust the future. The more you are actively and proactively engaged the more successful you will be.

What is My Worst-Case Scenario?

By way of analogy, we may compare your situation with the process of risk management.

The worst case is not frightening, not knowing is frightening. If you do not succeed, then try again and again – and then stop acting like a complete fool.[28] The concept of Situational Leadership is very important, especially in times like these with profound shifts in the global power balance and in the balance between the private and the public sectors.[29] It is simply necessary – for you as well – to try another leadership style, rather than carrying on with more of the same. Leadership used to be about seeking continuity, then it became reacting to changes and now it has become creating change. It is important to manage the journey and not only to focus on the destination. We need to act as leaders instead of playing defense.

Risk Management is the process which measures or evaluates risks and develops strategies to tackle them. The potential strategies include transfer of risk to another party, avoidance of risk, reduction of the negative effect of the risk and acceptance of some or all consequences of a specific risk. Formerly, risk management focused exclusively on physical and legal risks which you can insure yourself against (e.g., natural catastrophes, fire, death, or legal proceedings). Then financial risk management came along and focused on the risks that can be dealt with through the balanced use of financial instruments. In recent years more and more focus has been directed towards market risk management. This deals with ensuring the continuity of the business and hence the continued success of the corporation when (and not if) market conditions change significantly. Market risk management consists of revealing a complex network of risks related to business strategies, investment flexibility, navigating in market upheavals and, not least, a comprehensive communicative preparedness. Enterprise risk management seems to be the current most developed risk management. The market has 100 million brains and 200 million eyes – why do you think you are smarter?

Our minds are not equipped to handle the massive live digital coverage of natural catastrophes, acts of terror, war, rebellions, cultural, and demographic shifts, economic crime, industrial espionage, hacked IT systems, technological breakthroughs, and new communication platforms that set the complex agenda of today. Therefore, it is necessary to fight the state of permanent alert that your body senses. It is beneficial to reduce the concept of your personal risk to a manageable and realistic dimension. Risks are a measure of people. People who refuse to take them are trying to preserve what they have. People who do take risks often end up having more power, wealth, and happiness. The greatest risk of all is the risk of self-limitation.

Flemming's Tale: Building Flemming 7.0

Flemming realized that he had completed six versions of himself – he was now building Flemming 7.0. He had worked in a ministry, an association of lawyers and economists, a pension fund, a mortgage institution, a back-office administration, and a philanthropic fund – but he had never been an entrepreneur! Flemming discovered that he was highly motivated by intellectual stimulus and that he enjoyed structuring and simplifying complexity. He felt challenged by changing perspective (mentally, socially, culturally, linguistically or geographically). He also documented that he liked to use humor and have fun. It became evident that he wanted to focus on content rather than income. He wanted to build on his integrated social, financial, administrative, and political platform. His worst case scenario was that the people he wanted to talk to didn't want to talk to him. Another worst case scenario was that his grand project should remain a mirage.

Jan's Tale: Building Jan 3.0

Jan realized that he had had two home runs: One as a Partner in Grant Thornton and one as a Partner in BDO. He was now working on Jan 3.0 = The Senior Controller with the aim of creating Jan 4.0 = The Chief Financial Officer (CFO). Success for Jan was to make others benefit from his actions, to convert theory into practice, feel responsible and challenged, and enjoy freedom. People often described him as a "we-person" – he was an excellent team leader and everybody wanted to work for him. In that way he was a role model. His talent pipeline was excellent and the professional level in his team was great. He also found out that he was significantly better at providing help to others rather than himself asking for help. He was at his best when he had some difficult projects to handle, as it allowed him to combine his analytical skills and his solid overview. As he put it: "A manager looks at the bottom line; a leader looks at the horizon".

Key Learning

- Be explicit about your limits – keep your promises towards yourself.
- Eliminate wishful thinking – make a reality check.
- Paint a clear picture of your success – both personally and professionally.
- Document your dreams in writing – and they will materialize.
- Believe in what you're doing – or start doing something else.
- Take a risk – the worst outcome is seldom as bad as you fear.
- Celebrate your victories – you have more glorious moments than you think.
- Be honest towards yourself – explicitly state your deep down motivation.
- Trust your inner voice – it often knows the answer to your dilemmas.
- Define what is important in your life – and do your utmost to preserve it.

4

What Energizes Me?

> *//* Great minds discuss ideas;
> Average minds discuss events;
> Small minds discuss people *//*
> *Eleanor Roosevelt*

A competency is an underlying characteristic of an individual that is causally related to superior performance in a job. It is a measurable characteristic related to success at work and can consist of knowledge, skills, and attributes.

In the context of *The Personal Business Plan* it is important to underline that a competency follows you – it is your competency. This means that by increasing your competencies and becoming more competent, you create value for yourself. So here we are talking leadership for your lifetime, not for your specific job. It is also important to stress that some competencies are simply price of admission competencies, which are common to most people. You must get rid of the usual suspects and differentiate yourself. You must find out in which competencies you excel and clearly formulate those in order to create your competitive advantage.

Sometimes it may be useful to use a simple framework to identify your leadership mode. The management guru Ichak Adizes has developed the popular PAEI framework of prototypical management styles: Producer, Administrator, Entrepreneur, and Integrator. The two dimensions covered are Extrovert/Introvert and Emotions/Documentation.[30]

Table 3 The PAEI Framework of Prototypical Management Styles

	EXTROVERT	INTROVERT
DOCUMENTATION	PRODUCER	ADMINISTRATOR
EMOTIONS	ENTREPRENEUR	INTEGRATOR

Neil LaChapelle in *The Structure of Concern – A Challenge for Thinkers*[31] proposes the following definitions:

⬦ **Producers** are high energy people, active and extrovert. They like to be busy all the time, and their interests are overwhelmingly concrete. They love to attain tangible results and feel highly rewarded each time they can declare a task complete.

⬦ **Administrators** are quiet, cautious people who are less concerned with what we should do than how we should do it. They are extremely uncomfortable with ambiguity or uncertainty, and they are made uneasy by unstructured environments and group reliance on spontaneity and improvisation.

⬦ **Entrepreneurs** are easily typecast as dreamers. They are not interested in the results we are attaining today and would rather focus on bigger potential achievements in the future. Entrepreneurs feel stifled by the demands of ongoing activities. The here-and-now is a trap. Entrepreneurs are talkative and charismatic. Sometimes, they should be careful with what they wish for – it might come true. Anyway, they always need to define an exit strategy.

⬦ **Integrators** are team-builders within the organization. They manage the interpersonal, interdepartmental, supplier, and client relationships that allow the organization to function together as one organic whole. They are less concerned about formal roles and titles and more concerned that people pull together. Therefore, they often perform hidden work, work that is only visible, if it is not done!

You might identify yourself (more or less) with one of these profiles. A management team must include all four roles if it is to be successful over time and in changing contexts. In order to establish your professional identity you need to identify your leadership DNA from a competency and work platform perspective. Other useful typologies could be the Myers-Briggs Type Indicator[32] or the Belbin Team Roles Framework.[33]

I would like to draw your attention in particular to two types of specific team roles related to creativity: *The Plant*, who is creative, imaginative, unorthodox, and good at solving difficult problems; and *The Resource Investigator*, who is extrovert, enthusiastic, communicative, and good at exploring opportunities. One without the other will not succeed and the most successful partnerships in business (and life) are typically examples of this constellation.

Building Your Professional Identity

Very often, the building of your professional identity takes place through a weaving process. You remake yourself as you grow and as the world changes. Your identity isn't just discovered. It emerges. You integrate inputs from role models, mentors, colleagues, and other people who are important to you. This is why your first bosses can be defining for your future career. If early in your career you are lucky enough to have an unselfish boss who sincerely wants you to grow and develop, then you are set for a positive circle where praise leads to self-confidence, which again leads to new initiatives and positive results. I can only encourage you to actively seek as much feedback as possible from bosses, colleagues, and family on an ongoing basis. Feedback is an act of love.

Dealing with ambiguity is a competency. Ambiguity tolerance and flexibility are much sought-after qualities that will prepare you for the unexpected. In this hyper-complex world we need to be able to take decisions based on limited information. We need to be able to adapt rapidly when the environment changes. And we need to take advantage of the windows of opportunities that we meet along our way. Sometimes this means slowing down, allowing our attention to identify polarities and dilemmas, and dwelling on fundamental issues in the present.

Sometimes it is a good idea to compare your professional life to your hobbies. Some people just pass time at the office but when they come home and are able to focus on their hobbies they are totally energized. Imagine what they could accomplish if they invested the same energy at work! However, I also have respect for people who go to work in order to deliver a concentrated effort and afterwards go home in order to be 100% with the family. This might even be a good long-term survival strategy.

Inspiration: Competency Perspective

The Association of Executive Search Consultants is the worldwide professional association for retained executive search firms. AESC has published a guide to career management called *Executive Search and Your Career*.[34] From a competency perspective, the following questions may help you:

- Are you a leader, follower, originator, executor, builder or maintainer?
- Do you work better with structured or less structured problems and environments?
- Do you prefer a large or small organization?
- Are you risk-averse or a risk taker?
- Are these traits reflected in your career so far and your plans for the future?
- What are your current skills (e.g. finance, marketing, selling, analysis, planning, creating, writing, speaking in public)?
- What skills do you most enjoy using?
- How would you rate your leadership skills?
- What skills would you like to have?

What are My Strengths?

*You cannot turn a pig into a racing horse;
the best you can get is a fast pig!*
Unknown

You can program yourself for success by running with your strengths. I would recommend studying the work of Donald O. Clifton and Marcus Buckingham from The Gallup Organization, 2001,[35] which discusses the value of focusing on your strengths and finding ways to work around your weaknesses. Become aware of what you can do and what you cannot.

Your efforts to compensate for your weaknesses or to become better at doing such tasks will not give the same return as if you were to accept what you are not good at and then stop doing it! All your energy should go towards utilizing your strengths to the maximum. This is where you differentiate yourself from the crowd and create a sustainable competitive advantage. Marcus Buckingham made another groundbreaking discovery when he found out that your strengths are not only what you master, but are also what give you energy.[36] This is an extremely interesting differentiator between interests and strengths. There may be one activity that you would define as your strength because you are competent at doing it and you find it easy or satisfying to carry out. The acid test is whether you feel energized by the activity. If it is truly one of your strengths, then you should feel more energetic after having carried it through than before. It can help you define your *real* key competencies and prepare your mind for imagining a future situation where you only focus on doing what you like and what you are excellent at.

> *If you are entering the valley of despair, don't set up camp!*
> *Unknown*

Creating Trust

I believe that trust creates results and that you, through your communication, can create energy. Furthermore, this goes for trust in yourself, trust in others, and trust in the future. You will soon feel the benefits of accentuating and dramatizing the positive at all times in your work and social dealings – after all, you never get a second chance to make a good first impression. You are competent – you have the solution in you – you already know this and you feel secure in this knowledge. This feeling of security and trust in your own self-worth will allow you to be generous in your treatment of others. The former President of The Coca-Cola Company, Robert W. Woodruff, stated that there is no limit to what a man can do or where he can go if he does not mind who gets the credit.[37] So be generous and charming in your social demeanor and behavior.

> *Charm can provide you with a way of getting the answer yes without having asked a specific question*
> *Albert Camus*[38]

If your organization were a person, would you like to be around it? It is not everyone who can answer this question positively and this is precisely why many companies have difficulties attracting and retaining talent. Three major dimensions emerge.

1. The Psychological Contract

The first central dimension regarding the attraction and retention of talent is whether the companies have broken the psychological contract with their employees through exaggerated use of downsizing, rightsizing, restructuring, delayering, and other euphemisms for personnel cutbacks and firing rounds. Earlier, the deal was that if the employee took employment, then the corporation would do everything in its power to earn the loyalty of that employee. In principle, in today's brutal business environment, everyone can be fired and the result is increasing degrees of galvanization for both the employee and the employer. The very concept of a company man might just be a thing of the past. One specific case comes to mind: An EMEA President of a global company was on holiday at the beach together with his two sons. He took a phone call that turned out to be from two lawyers from headquarters. The message was: "Sorry to inform you that you are not with the company anymore – it is not personal!"

2. Work-Life Balance

The second central dimension in attracting talent is work-life balance. Many corporations operate actively with the formulation of attractive terms of employment that also provide space for family and hobbies. The paradox is that the responsible employee is online most of the time simply because technological development has made it possible (and, thus, it is seen as necessary). In today's culture it is no longer natural to log off. You are on constant stand-by. In business life we see this most clearly with executives working across many time zones. Most of East Asia including China, Hong Kong. and Singapore is 12 hours ahead of New York; that gives long working days for executives with activities on more than one continent.

3. Sense of Urgency

A third important dimension focuses on whether these hyperactive 24/7 companies are, in reality, efficient. When the tempo is hiked up, transparency within the organization often suffers and the success criteria become unclear. In a well-known American IT corporation the average executive remains just eight months in one position – and then it is onwards and upwards. Not surprisingly, the new executive tends to focus on the short-term knowing that he or she will only have eight months to identify the issue *and* implement the solution. After that it is important to get a promotion before any negative effects of the action taken become visible.

According to the management guru Ram Charan[39], this trend also challenges the boards: Companies should have a deep pool of internal candidates, an updated and refined succession plan and a solid executive search process. For outgoing CEOs, the mean tenure shortened 18 months in a decade: 6.6 years in 2010 versus 8.1 in 2000.[40] In particular, the length of planned tenures – in which the CEO departs on a date that has been prearranged with the board – dropped by 30%, from 10 to 7 years. These findings suggest that CEOs are finding the demands of the job more pressing than their predecessors did. The consultancy firm Booz&Co has calculated that if this development continues at the same rate, a chief executive in 2042 will have an average tenure of one day!

In tackling any project go for intention, not perfection. Sometimes it is more important to prototype rapidly than to come up with the ideal solution. Cisco is one company that employs the 80% rule – finish the product, concept, or service up to 80%, release it internally and build all the resulting feedback into the ultimate product, concept, or solution. Never try to finish it by yourself – the efforts of and the qualitative input from the team and your network counts for much more than your personal, individual contribution. Always use the potential of your team and your competent network to the full and avoid creating your own self-limitations. Reid Hoffman, Co-founder and Chairman of LinkedIn, says it like this: "No matter how brilliant your mind or strategy, if you're playing a solo game, you'll always lose out to a team. I^{We} (I-to-the-We)."[41]

Flow

In order to reach your personal targets you need to prioritize and make some "to do" lists of action points towards which you feel committed. Remember that it takes both stamina and patience – even if you try pulling at a carrot in the ground, it will not grow any faster. Some of the personality traits that you will certainly need are: Authenticity, integrity, robustness and ambition. You may also need to try an alternative approach to solving problems.

For most people it is relatively simple to target their strengths. If a feeling of success, wellbeing or happiness occurs in relation to a certain activity then it is probably one of your strengths. "*Flow*" is a central concept when looking for your strengths. If you have ever found yourself in a state of flow at your work then you were surely using one of your strengths – and it is highly probable that you were exceptionally productive at that time.

It is all about maximizing the number of "flow situations" and minimizing the number of "overflow situations", where your challenges overwhelm you. When

I come home after a day of lecturing at Copenhagen Business School, my wife often comments on my good mood. OK, then I can tick off teaching as one of my strengths. I thrive on teaching and even though it demands a lot of effort both before and during the lectures, it's all worth it: Because when you use your strengths it gives you more energy. The triple gain – increased productivity, better mood and increased energy – illustrates the fantastic potential when you succeed in focusing more on your strengths and less on your weaknesses.

Exercise: Your Building Blocks

I would now like you to reflect on how your present job is in harmony with you as a person. Reflect on how the three following concepts are in harmony with each other:

- Your personal values
- Your competencies
- The tasks that you solve.

Try looking at the following illustrations, which I have chosen to call the "Jenga model" after the classic children's game, where the players use oblong blocks to build a tower – and then start removing them one by one until the tower becomes so unstable that it falls over.

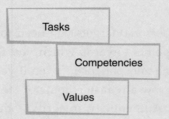

Sometimes your competencies are not aligned with the tasks and your values. In the previous example, however, the tasks are aligned with your values.

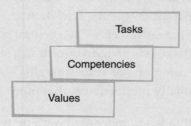

In the previous model there is no alignment between your tasks, your competencies, and your values. Of course this creates serious imbalance, tension, and conflict.

Now I would like you to point at a situation, a project or a course of action where you experienced *harmony* between the three levels of the model. Where the model looked like this:

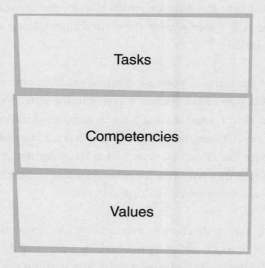

The described process or project is probably one of the times when you have been the closest to a professional ideal condition. I am sure that you look back at the time with joy and pride. Again, it is worth going back to the wellbeing analysis earlier in Your Personal Business Plan where you have probably touched upon relevant experiences.

Remember that the ideal relationship between a certain task and your competencies is *not* that the task was easy for you – but that it was sufficiently hard to contribute to your development.

We all know people, who apparently have an extra gear; who seemingly work more than others and always are in a good mood and radiate energy. When I meet executives who thrive at working hard many hours per week I often ask them to draw the model. It *always* becomes clear that there is harmony between their values, their competencies and their tasks. People whose *Jenga model* is in harmony are perceived as perpetual motion machines. They can work around the clock.

Don't simply point out a time where the situation was ideal for you. Pay attention thoroughly to the details, that created the situation, and describe the positive experiences you had in the process.

If you arrange your life so that you continuously experience situations where the three parameters come together then you will experience victories in a row. You will create maximum value for yourself and your organization, and during the process you will experience a flow condition whose energy will spread to the rest of your life.

When you have formulated your ideal situation then you will experience that your Personal Business Plan makes it possible for you to execute the success experience. You don't need to wait for a similar situation to occur, which perhaps will never happen. Because you now have a target it becomes possible for you to recreate the circumstances which have earlier created an ideal situation in your life. In this way you have become less dependent of coincidences and have taken a step towards lifelong success.

What works for you will change throughout life. Everything is in constant motion and what works excellently now will not necessarily do so in the future. You may try adjusting your ambition level but at some point in time you will probably need to seek challenges elsewhere in order to obtain the same effect. But not necessarily! Before going on stage, President Bill Clinton says – mostly to himself – "It's show time, folks!" You can clearly see that he still feels an intense joy by being in a situation that he defines as ideal.

Inspiration: Time Perspective

The global negotiation trainer Richard R. Gesteland has pointed out the difference between *monochronic* (rigid) and *polychronic* (fluid) time behavior.[42] People in some of the world's business cultures worship the clock, while others are relaxed about deadlines and schedules. Negotiators from monochronic cultures who tend to think and plan sequentially are frequently frustrated when faced with typical polychronic attitudes which correspond to multitasking or surprising changes in the negotiating procedure.

> // Your mind is like a parachute,
> it only works when it is open //
> *Unknown*

An open mind is a learning mind – you automatically gain new insights. You should, therefore, seek to transform any situation into a learning situation. In your interactions with others ask open-ended questions and listen to the answers. Look for useful mirrors in those around you; look at yourself and change behavior. Above all, dare to see and acknowledge your blind spots. All learning presupposes a prior recognition of your lack of ability or understanding. Most people like having learned, but do not enjoy learning. In future society knowledge will be the most important resource and lifelong learning the most important process. *Learning Agility* is the single best predictor of high-potential talent and sustained success. It is primordial for your success in work and in life that you become able at discerning when you are confronted to something new and accepting that you have to react in a different manner than usual. Learn what to do when you don't know what to do. Never just more of the same!

It might be a good idea for you to look at your life through the following lenses: Function, Behavior, and Person.

Most often, it would be advantageous for you to dissociate your function, your behavior, and your person from each other. Imagine that your function and your behavior become synonymous. Then you will be reduced to a bureaucrat who only does what is dictated by the function. Now imagine that your behavior and your person become synonymous. Then you will be seen as a freewheeling molecule with no respect for your environment.

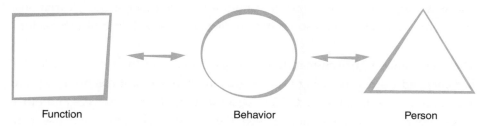

Function   Behavior   Person

Figure 10 Function, Behavior, and Person

As you can clearly see the three geometrical forms "Square", "Circle", and "Triangle" are incommensurable. There is no way you can make two or three of the forms totally overlap in a harmonious way. So don't try! Some things are functional. Some things are behavioral. And some things are personal. They are not all three at the same time.

The trick is to fluently adapt to the different contexts that you meet – both acting in accordance with your values and respecting the norms of society. In my experience the biggest personal pain is felt when people take criticism personally, rather than as criticism of them as a function. However, most of the time, your behavior simply goes with the territory. You have a certain objective to reach and therefore you act in accordance with this goal. So next time when feeling stressed due to criticism, remember that it has probably nothing to do with you. Behave constructively and independently of the signals of guilt and shame that your subconscious sends you. Deal with the situation at hand. Go into functional mode and solve the problem.

If you have both a strong body and a strong mind, your robustness and drive will help you reach your goals. Many leaders I have met run marathons and meditate. They explain that these activities help them to focus and be stress-resistant. They gain a better insight into themselves and, thus, are able to act with more strength and authenticity. Strong individuals more easily show kindness and understanding, and they have the surplus mental and physical energy to assist others.

The same leaders also tell me that the discipline of training prepares them for adversity. If they think the training is hard, they are forgetting how tough they are – and it is important that they have chosen to make this extra effort themselves. Some of us may know the proverb, *When the going gets tough, the tough get going*. Even though this thought was adopted into the popular culture of the 1980s and was subjected to numerous (and humorous) "bumper sticker" variations, experience seems to demonstrate that, in fact, adversity does build character.

The management guru Sumantra Ghoshal[43] stated that the role of the leader has changed from structuring tasks to shaping behaviors. It has become more and more demanding for the CEO to be a role model for employees and other stakeholders. If a CEO does not succeed, the younger generations will use their collective thumb and vote with their feet.

Several times I have worked with leaders who have their own role models. When, together with me, they meticulously go through and map the competencies and the personal qualities that characterize their role models they suddenly realize that they themselves have all the same leadership characteristics and character traits. In other words they have become their own role models and hence they have themselves become role models. It makes a huge difference in their lives to perceive themselves as role models instead of seeking to emulate former role models. And hence one more self-limitation disappears. Try now to look at yourself as a role model and accept deep down that you are an exemplary individual. It might be that you don't have to look so hard for the perfect behavior. It might be that you are already well on your way and that other people look up to you, perhaps even without you knowing it.

Inspiration: Culture Perspective

Jim Collins writes in *Built to Last*[44] that successful companies are those which succeed in growing an exceptional position by gathering the whole organization around its purpose and key values. More and more, the role of the chief executive is to influence the corporate culture so that energy is directed outwards – outside the organization – and not inwards. In the knowledge-based society, successful business models use less financial capital and more human capital; it is crucial, therefore, that employees reflect and signal the values of the corporation in their actions and activities. One of the most difficult tasks for a growing organization is to maintain the family feeling of the smaller organization and to provide a nurturing environment for the desired culture of the company. Without this environment, the culture of the organization may veer off course with potentially damaging consequences. Employees must identify with the culture of the company as envisaged by top management and use it to guide their actions. In the final analysis, culture is what people do when nobody tells them what to do.

What are My Weaknesses?

Ask yourself the question "What do I desperately want to change about myself?" Do not despair, to change is easy if you are decided and committed. The difficult part is taking the active and conscious decision. As soon as you have defined your primary weaknesses you will be free to make the bungee jump of your life. And please remember that what got you here, won't get you there. Are you the way you want to be? Do you have a good conscience? Do you feel good?

We cling to the notion that there is a constant inside of us – an unchanging core that follows us despite all the other changes we may undergo – and which we often refer to as "A self". Because we perceive this self as vulnerable, we do all we can in order to protect and please it. We feel disgust for everything that threatens it and feel drawn towards everything that confirms or pleases it. But it is when we cling to this self that the problems arise. Buddhists call it attachment. We think that we are our self. We defend it with all means at our disposal. When somebody threatens us, we feel anger and we retaliate. When we desire something or somebody, we want to own it or them. The Buddhists' response to attachment is meditation; a fully conscious attempt to sit and just observe thought and emotions come and go. As many – also non-Buddhist – practitioners of meditation have experienced by doing this you can improve your general state of mind.

Inspiration: Empty Bowl Perspective

You can work very effectively with the symbol of the empty bowl. It was first introduced to me in an executive group where a facilitator held something in his hand. He then asked us: "What is this?" We all came up with suggestions and described it in many ways. After a prolonged discussion we agreed that it was an empty bowl. When you describe a situation you describe an empty bowl. It is only when you add your emotions that the bowl is filled. And then you no longer focus on the empty bowl, but on its contents. So, as soon as we bring our own perceptions, emotions, prejudices or other filters into play, we reduce our effectiveness in observing, describing and focusing. This is also valid for leadership. Remember, that the success of an intervention depends on the interior condition of the intervener.

In order to free leadership energy you must be able to observe and listen to the surroundings without letting too many emotions come into play. You may compare it to observing an empty bowl. The bowl is the object and the emotions are what you put in the bowl. In other words, it is not the problem per se that is the problem but, rather, what you think about the problem that is the problem. Be conscious of the fact that you can choose to accord greater or lesser importance to any event. It is fundamental to be able to choose not to be affected by external circumstances.

Remember that sunk costs are just that – sunk. There is no need for wishful thinking about unrealistic dreams. You must build on your strengths and your competencies. And if you have taken a career path that is not fulfilling, you must change yet again in order to get the best out of the situation. What is difficult? What hurts? Focus on your short-term pain in order to benefit from your long term gain. It is human nature to avoid confronting bad news and to imagine that today's troubles will pass more quickly and easily than they really will. We all exhibit a tendency towards cocooning in times of crisis. Individuals, groups, and organizations tend to focus inwards and concentrate on the good stuff – reminiscing, for example, about how nice and cozy it was in the old days. In times of crisis the leadership perspective is to assume conditions will be worse than you actually expect – assume the worst case scenario. Scenario writing takes the drama and the acuteness and the tension out of the situation – it is not personal.

> *If you want to measure your importance in this world,*
> *stick your finger into a glass of water,*
> *take it out and see the mark you have left behind!*
> *Unknown*

Don't Seek Perfection

You need to accept the fact that you are not perfect. Just pretend you are human. In order to be an authentic leader you must confront your own incompetence. And we all suffer from unconscious incompetence: We don't know what we don't know. Sometimes, executive search consultants talk about *résumé-gods* who are excellent at performing a role created by the people and society around them, but have limited self-awareness. This means that they will inevitably reach their level of incompetence. If you know yourself, you have no enemies. When you have difficulties addressing an issue, focus on the why. In their book, *Just Enough: Tools for Creating Success in Your Work and Life,* Laura Nash and Howard Stephenson point out that "You cannot maximize two things if they are tradeoffs, by the very definition of maximizing. Limitation is built into the human condition. The only fixed time frame we know for sure is death. Everything else is subject to moving targets".[45]

In life, everybody is looking for long-term, quick fixes. These are very difficult to come by, but acting upon your fundamental principles will bring you a long way. The exercise of compassion works like a medicine that gives you back your serenity when you are anxious or overwrought. Leadership is "daring to step into the unknown", as the world-renowned theoretical physicist Stephen Hawking puts it. And I would add that leadership and running a business is a multi-lens activity in which you continuously must trust yourself. Robert S. Kaplan, Baker Foundation Professor at the Harvard Business School, introduced the 80/20/30 rule:[46] When you calculate cumulative profit as a function of the number of customers, you realize that the last 30% of your customers generate a loss that reduces the profit from the 20% most profitable customers. This means that you would be better off without this 30%. One of the reasons behind this finding is probably that top sales people are conflict averse, they don't like to say no, they prefer to please – so they don't stop selling!

A similar concept could be applied to a strength/weakness analysis – if taken too far, your strengths can become weaknesses. Robert E. Kaplan (not to be confused with the previously mentioned Robert S. Kaplan) and Robert B. Kaiser wrote an intriguing *Harvard Business Review* article: "Stop Overdoing Your Strengths".[47] They document that there is a permanent and significant risk linked to overdoing your strengths. Continued 360-degree feedback does not capture overkill and more is not necessarily better. Ask yourself "Do I privately pride myself on being superior to other leaders in any way?" If this is the case, this is precisely the attribute you are at risk of overdoing. If you are not sure of the answer, ask your spouse, partner, children or close friend who will probably know. The former French president, Charles de Gaulle, commented: "Genius . . . sometimes consists of knowing when to stop."

Use the following SWOT Analysis to document your strengths and weaknesses and work at identifying where associated opportunities and threats lie. Be wary of strengths that may conceal future threats and pay particular attention to signature strengths that can be turned into existential opportunities. This SWOT analysis should provide you with a useful tool to document what you can achieve and which areas you should focus on. A general guideline is: Focus on your strengths and exercise damage control on your weaknesses.

Just for the record: 85% of all interviewees name impatience as a weakness. So if you want to differentiate yourself from the other candidates, don't go down that road!

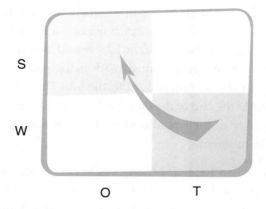

Figure 11 Personal SWOT Analysis

What is My Passion?

Inspiration: Passion Perspective

From a passion perspective, the following questions from AESC's *Career Management Guide*[48] might help you:

- What do you feel deeply about?
- What excites you?
- What would you do if you did not have to work for a living?
- Can you make a career, and a living, out of your passion?

I want you to experience a feeling of freedom and independence – just like Pinocchio with no strings holding you down – not even the umbilical cord. Imagine yourself working with a landline telephone. You may be able to remember when you were not able to move beyond a certain radius because the cord was always in the way, holding you back. Then came wireless and with it mobility. Nowadays it is difficult to imagine not being reachable and individually available around the clock. Back then, the liberating effect of technology was often exaggerated; a commonly asked question was: "What shall we do with all the free time we will have on our hands?" In contrast BSA (Bandwidth Separation Anxiety) is now a well-known phenomenon among executives. Many admit that they feel better when they have constant access to all information and all business contacts. Mails flow continuously through the smartphone or the laptop and the executives are always available. It is likely that future generations will react against this constant job-related floating attention. Many young people, even today, react against work being such a dominant part of the identity; they cut the umbilical cord to the job. They do not define themselves by their jobs. At the end of the day, it is them and their family and friends. They judge the quality of their relationships by their sense of belonging – the cohesiveness of the moment.

Ambitious people have a tendency to say yes to new challenges and that adds layer upon layer of competencies. The only problem is that they very often forget to get rid of the competencies that do not serve them anymore. This means that their self-image does not correspond to what is optimal judged from a future perspective – they are not necessarily projecting the image that will propel them even further along their chosen path. Very often this has to do with pride; it is difficult to say goodbye to competencies for which you have previously been praised and which have contributed significantly to your present success. But it is necessary:

- ⊗ Old habits are your enemies.
- ⊗ Inventiveness has become the order of the day.
- ⊗ Creativity is the key to new energy – your second wind.
- ⊗ Break your habits and identify new patterns in your brain.
- ⊗ Say goodbye to your old friends.
- ⊗ Kill your darlings.
- ⊗ Your nostalgia kills your happiness.

These simple sentences will help you morph into a new and improved you. If you accept and act upon them, you will have left behind some of the driftwood that prevented you from taking a deep dive into your passion. Too often, business people work within bounded rationality. I am building on the notion of passion in order to maximize human potential and release energy.

Rhetorical Styles

You may be inspired by Aristotle's *Three Main Rhetorical Styles*: Ethos – Logos – Pathos. *Ethos* is appeal based on the character of the speaker. *Logos* is appeal based on logic or reason. *Pathos* is appeal based on emotion. So activating your Pathos is the key to finding your professional passion. Sometimes intuition, that is, the sum of your experience, is the keystone to understanding the world around us. Our brains have a certain capacity for detecting regularity to the extent that when the world matches these characteristics, we see structure and pattern. However, when behavior in the world exceeds our capacities, the excess of sophistication is lost on us and turns into randomness, into an apparent lack of structure that we cannot represent.[49]

The theory of multiple intelligences was developed in *Frames of Mind* in 1983 by Dr Howard Gardner, Professor of Education at Harvard University.[50] It suggested that the traditional notion of intelligence, based on IQ testing, is far too limited. Instead, Dr Gardner proposed seven new intelligences to account for a broader range of human potential. These intelligences are:

- Verbal/Linguistic ("word smart")
- Logical/Mathematical ("reasoning smart")
- Visual/Spatial ("picture smart")
- Bodily/Kinesthetic ("body smart")
- Musical ("music smart")
- Interpersonal ("people smart")
- Intrapersonal ("self-smart")

We all know successful soccer or football players. The best among them have a feeling for the game that is simply amazing. They cannot explain how they do it, but they feel compelled to be at exactly the right moment at precisely the right place. They integrate their perception of time and space instantly and know exactly where the ball will be. Their kinesthetic intelligence allows them to act on this knowledge and influence the future through their intervention.

Flemming's Tale: Key Competencies

Flemming is now building up his preparative efforts and, without knowing it yet, is starting to create the foundation of what will later become his Catalytic Society concept. He focuses on the following Key Competencies: Societal Interest, Ambiguity Tolerance, Financial Acumen, Empowering Leadership, Organizational

Integration, Stakeholder Management, Political Ingenuity, Governance Model, Global Inspiration, and Strategic Philanthropy. By this he means that he has an intense interest in society, he is intrigued by diversity and handles it well, he is very reliable in financial matters, he delegates and gives room, he makes the different business units collaborate, he has a clear view of the self-interest of each stakeholder, he looks through many political schemes, he does things by the book, he seeks inspiration all over the world and he is thrilled by the future of capitalism: Capitalism 5.0.

Already at this point in his Personal Business Plan process he has formulated many of the key concepts that he will later use as building blocks for his Life Ambition.

Jan's Tale: Key Competencies

Jan defined one of his key strengths as being a good human being. He possessed a strong mental attitude – which he called his sixth gear. Jan was reflecting and thoughtful – fair and demanding. He had always worked hard in a disciplined and structured way. He preferred sticking to the truth, which had served him well. He had had a tendency towards perfectionism and self-critical behavior. Gradually, through his work with his Personal Business Plan, this turned into a sense of self-esteem and pride. He described his goodwill among employees, peers and bosses as his Career Capital. Jan would like to improve his courage and his patience with other people. Sometimes he also felt that he was not friendly enough – inadvertently being rude – especially when he was focused and deep in his own thoughts. One of the major themes of his Personal Business Plan emerged here: He suddenly realized that other people are not mind readers. They had to be told what Jan thought. Jan confided that he was very seldom surprised by what other people told him – he had already been through most of the conversations in his mind. However, this introvert key competency doesn't work the other way round!

Key Learning

- Define the competencies that differentiate you from the crowd.
- Describe your best fit with Producer, Administrator, Entrepreneur or Integrator.
- Identify your strengths – remember that a strength energizes you.
- Learn what to do when you don't know what to do.
- Exercise dealing with volatility, uncertainty, complexity and ambiguity.
- Focus on what you're excellent at.
- Trust yourself, trust others and trust your future.
- Discipline yourself and train for adversity – adversity builds character.
- Pretend to be human – paint a picture that looks like you.
- Ask yourself "Do I privately pride myself on being superior to other leaders in any way?"

5

Where am I on My Personal Journey?

"Leading from the future as it emerges"
Claus Otto Scharmer

For many years I have had the privilege of working with both excellent business professionals and excellent business psychologists. The quality of the solutions provided in the field of tension between these two competencies can be breathtaking. My wife once pointed out that my learning about the "soft" side of human capital is the best thing that ever happened in our marriage.

Psychologists have the huge advantage of knowing the generalized life pattern of an individual in advance. They can therefore work deductively by comparing to a norm or an expected typical behavior. Others have to generalize from their own experiences and, by trial and error, reach their own conclusions through an inductive process. There can be no doubt that the former process is the more effective for understanding human behavior.

To be in the cross field between psychology and business – the combination of the soft and the hard – is exciting. We all consider ourselves unique. However, as the psychologist Carl Rogers has found, what is most personal is also most general.[51] Deep down we share the same fears and the same doubts. We all want to be loved; we all fear solitude. During different periods of our life we suffer similar concerns. All of us pass the same milestones on our safari through life (*safari* means journey in Swahili). The most extraordinary experience awaits you just around the bend if you are open to it. This openness or curiosity of mind will lead you to realize that when you are in doubt, you are, in fact, not in doubt. Sometimes, by practicing personal disclosure and openly telling about your doubts, they simply disappear.

Where am I in My Life?

Let's start with you. In order to identify your place in the greater picture it would be useful to discover your relevant lifecycle phase. Many scholars have built on the work of Rudolf Steiner who, in the early twentieth century, conceived of a theory of human development based upon seven-year cycles[52]:

Table 4 My Life Phases

Age (years)	Description
0–7	Phase 1: Strong desire to learn
7–14	Phase 2: Critical and rebellious
14–21	Phase 3: Strong need to build an identity
21–28	Phase 4: Need to settle down
28–35	Phase 5: Ego-driven – "Been there, seen it & done it!"
35–42	Phase 6: "Who am I?" – More philosophical perspective
42–49	Phase 7: "How can I do it again?" – Need to resettle down (mirror phase 4)
49–56	Phase 8: Need to re-establish an identity (mirror phase 3)
56–63	Phase 9: Again critical and rebellious (mirror phase 2)
63–70+	Phase 10: Again a strong desire to learn (mirror phase 1)

Source: Rudolph Steiner

It can, of course, be argued that such strict chronological cycles as described in Table 4 are neither universal nor transcendent of time. Current urban myth (heavily promoted by the advertising industry and media) tells us that "40 is the new 30" and so on. Even so, based on experience, I would suggest that by the time you reach 50 years of age, you have developed a totally different perspective on relationships – including close personal relationships – than you held when you were, say, in your twenties. Most people in their fifties recognize that relationships are built on shared information and experiences and this may explain why people tend to become more tolerant of the people around them as they become older. Old friends may have developed some eccentricities over the years, but they are accepted and valued because of the treasure trove of shared memories.

> " Age is a question of mind over matter.
> If you don't mind, it doesn't matter. "
> *Leroy (Satchel) Paige*

When you consider your own life, you can be on one of two trajectories. One, where you feel energized and seek to utilize the synergies of your knowledge to the fullest: "Life goes on . . . life is good". Or the other, where you do not accept that your situation in life has been brought about by your own choices. The latter trajectory adheres to the Hobbesian view that "Life is nasty, brutish and short"[53] or, translated into the modern equivalent "Life's a bitch . . . and then you die!" If you are on the second life trajectory, your form of transformation is a sense of lost opportunities and an even deeper crystallization of long-held viewpoints. Your challenge is to identify on which trajectory you are – and seek to change it, if the long term perspective does not seem appealing. It is never too late to radically change your lifestyle, it simply takes some self-discipline. Over time you will become more of who you wish to be. Even though you may feel that time is not on your side, it is important to adopt a long time horizon. A Chinese philosopher was once asked to comment on Mao Zedong's Cultural Revolution. His answer was "It's too early. 1000 years from now we can tell".

Creativity

In order to move from where and what you are to where and who you want to be, you will need to draw on your own creativity. Art is what makes you ask questions you didn't know you were going to ask. Creativity springs from many sources. It is interesting to note that different professionals, whether they are artists, scientists or consultants, all describe the creative process in the same way – as being able to see oneself in the picture, being aware of one's own objective influence on the observed item, and seeing both the whole and the parts.

Paul Arden, former Executive Creative Director of Saatchi & Saatchi, has described life's creative circle in the following way:[54]

Table 5 Life's Creative Circle

Age (years)	Description
0–5	Minimalism and fantasy
5–10	The beginning of copying
10–15	Art becomes grown up
15–20	A need to change the world
20–25	Beginnings of political awareness
25–30	Maturity
30–40	Hell bent on success
40–45	Repeating success
45–50	Trying to keep up with the 25-year-olds
50	The watershed
50–60	Reinventing yourself
60–75	A gentle decline into senility
75–85	Youth regained
85–100	Inhibitions lost. Don't give a damn. Me, me, me.

Source: Paul Arden

The elementary aesthetic areas of children, naïve, forgetful, and inexperienced people are intact early in life. Due to their lack of routine they easily wonder about the world. So there is a childlike quality to keeping your aesthetic urge: Your ability to wonder, your craving for novelty and opportunities, for acting on impulse, for acting now, spontaneously with little or no thought for the possible consequences, acting positively instead of reacting negatively. The ability to retain this childlike enthusiasm is called staying young. Think about it: You are not as young as you used to be. But you are not as old as you are going to be. So watch it! Allow for change. You need to realize that you are already a dinosaur. But there is still hope that you may become an agile and nimble dinosaur!

The maturation process of an individual occurs in phases, and the transition from one phase to the next involves a qualitative change in consciousness. According to Robert Kegan, Professor in Adult Learning and Professional Development at Harvard Graduate School of Education, the identity of a human being is formed through a lifelong movement between personal experiences, relationships with other people, thoughts and reflections.[55] The ability to create meaning from one's fundamental identity, earlier experiences and the continuous influence of the surroundings is central to all human beings.

It reminds me of the mother of a colleague, who said: "Now I have been a wife, a mother, a grandmother for 87 years, can't I just be Karen?" Kegan argues that while each individual is unique we continually seek to fit into a given context. This results in a lifelong developmental spiral from a normativity level over an authority level to an integrity level:

- ⊗ At the **normativity level**, we download norms and act within their boundaries.
- ⊗ At the **authority level**, we slowly see ourselves as co-creators of meaning and direction – as an authority. In this context, authority means the ability to take responsibility both for ourselves and for others. It helps us set a solid context, goal, direction and a purposeful target.
- ⊗ At the **integrity level**, we are able to discern similarity hidden behind what we perceived as differences before. We are able to see differences as well as likeness in the same process, because we understand both ourselves and others – despite any apparent contradictions. When we reach the integrity level, we are able to handle paradoxes and relate constructively to contradictions. Our tolerance of ambiguity is higher and our leadership is more authentic.

In terms of energy levels most people peak in their thirties. The combination of energy and experience culminates between 35 and 40 usually leading to a professional peak in this life phase. Sometimes this appears as a sprint whereas people in their forties may show a steadier stride. From 50 years and upwards many feel a greater need to mentor and help others. You may compare the human lifecycle of childhood, youth, maturity, and old age to the changing seasons of spring, summer, autumn and winter.

> *Better light your candle*
> *than curse the darkness*
> *Chinese proverb*

Interestingly, the often discussed "mid-life crisis" does seem to have some basis in fact. So while your professional life may be progressing swimmingly in your forties, this may coincide with the period in your life when you feel least happy. According to a report in the magazine *The Economist* (December 2010) the global average "happiness" nadir is at the age of 46.[56] But with increasing years most people also experience increasing happiness. So you can look forward to becoming not only an agile and nimble dinosaur, but also a happy dinosaur!

Find a Partner

One of the best ways of keeping ahead in business and in life is to find a partner. A Dynamic Duo provides a perspective on all aspects of life and forces you to reason and argue for your solutions to complex problems. Thus the problem solving process becomes more qualitative and grounded – a sort of reality check. It is not very difficult to agree on the best solution if you are pondering the problem alone at home in your study. Sometimes your partner in life becomes your business partner – at least in terms of discussing problems and solutions, situations, and possible outcomes. Being part of a partnership team seems to be an essential element of success. When asked why I have never divorced, my answer is that we never had the time, we never had the money, and neither of us wanted the children.

In his book *Outliers – The Story of Success*, Malcolm Gladwell mentions that most people agree that autonomy, complexity and a connection between effort and reward are the three qualities that work must have if it is to be satisfying.[57] I have certainly found this to be true which is why I have reinvented myself periodically by moving from one area of business activity to another: Fast Moving Consumer Goods, Professional Services, Lecturer, Headhunter, Coach, and Author. Reinvention brings with it new challenges, inspires new curiosity and the thirst for knowledge and understanding of the new activity area, and demands a close examination of where you are and where you are going. Reinvention – by avoiding boredom and awakening childlike enthusiasm – helps to prevent mental and physical "burn out" and, thus, is the key to longevity. You should, however, always keep the best from the past – pivoting on the fundamental qualities in your life. It is like a cultural DNA which encourages a rhythm of constant reinvention.

In order to liberate yourself and free up your leadership power, you need to decide which fundamental principles you want to follow in your life. As the Roman emperor Marcus Aurelius said: "Become who you are". Identify what you want to stand for and choose the strengths that you will consistently focus on. Cultivate your key competency and your specificity. Pick really distinctive ideas. Find your own voice and create your own reality.

What keeps so many of us from fully embracing personal leadership? My experience is that we all have barriers which we must fight to break through and reach beyond before we dare to stand by our own identity as leaders. In our memory we have printed a picture of our strengths and weaknesses, and we continue to believe in this picture even when our behavior and actions belie it. A top executive once told me that he was very shy and introvert. I had never perceived him as such and, therefore, it was a rather limiting self-image. Many executives adopt an extroverted persona in their professional dealings – even though they do not feel comfortable with this at first. It is simply a precondition for effectively representing an organization to its stakeholders.

Further, as a leader you need to enter into trustful dialogues where you give something of yourself. I believe in the value of meaningful dialogues. They tend to create the third road, not mine or yours, but ours. It is immensely important to be an interesting dialogue partner. It is rewarding to discover that you share opinions with people whose pathway to that point of view has been different from yours. It is both a form of validation and a reality check. It also provides cultural diversity. If you do not connect with other people, you do not create value for your organization or yourself. This connection enables you to gain insight and inspiration that you would otherwise lack. And, it should be remembered, insight involves more than intellect: Great people talk about ideas; average people talk about themselves; small people talk about others.

One comment from one of my mentors has left a permanent mark: "When the others are throwing sand at each other, don't climb into the sandbox!" I was truly delighted (and flattered) by a passing comment from a dear and close colleague with whom I have worked for many years. She told me that she had never heard me badmouth anybody. To me this is like a medal of distinction and it makes me very proud.[58]

Trust is the new currency of the digital age. The challenge in the current environment is to establish a relevant dialogue. An authentic relationship is often characterized by identification – where we feel that we are part of something bigger. In this situation consumption, for example, becomes a statement of who we are. Consumers and customers want to experience trust: They want to be understood, they want to be respected, and they want to be listened to. They certainly do not want to be talked at. If a message to consumers and customers is to reach its destination, it must be communicated on their terms and through their preferred channels. The present day consumer has a new mindset and this necessitates a new self-understanding in the corporation, anchored in the future and not in the past. Companies today seek to understand the consumer by the use of focus groups, advisory consumer panels and similar techniques. In the old days, characterized by one-way communication, companies had an information department!

What are My Personal Priorities?

You are your own project. Therefore you may as well create a meaningful project for yourself. In *Business Stripped Bare*, Richard Branson states this idea rather more provocatively: "Think about your financial life, your professional qualifications or your health. Are you confronting reality or are you living in 'la-la land'? Work on being completely honest with yourself. Take on the challenge of realigning your life with the principles that will create the results you want to have".[59]

Executives have traditionally busied themselves with answering the questions what? and how? But there is fantastic power buried in the question why? In Japan, you bow for a good question; you do not bow for a good answer. There lies a great untapped strength in not knowing all the answers. In return, most executives find it hard to express their doubts and insecurities in order to work together with the team to challenge the usual mental pictures and provoke optimal conclusions. But this is a barrier well-worth overcoming: So-called "dumb" questions often create greater clarity and thereby more valuable solutions.

What is My Potential for Personal Growth?

It is always possible to raise the bar and exploit opportunities by identifying new challenges. At the basis of all experience is the need for commitment and responsibility, not least towards yourself. Just for starters, try these five commandments:

⊗ Seek opportunities before anything else,
⊗ Take responsibility for your mood and your behavior,
⊗ Be thankful for what works,
⊗ Create moments of joy, and
⊗ Give time for reflection.

I would also suggest fishing where the big fish are. More often than not you will be able to detect new opportunities by listening to what is *not* being said. This skill of active listening is not an activity you can delegate. You need to proactively and constantly scan the market for new personal growth opportunities. So remember to leave room for capitalizing on unanticipated opportunities that emerge in day-to-day events.

Analyses are very useful within the so-called mechanical paradigm. This old paradigm is where we look at a known universe with known behavior. Where time is money, where safety is good, where change is dangerous, where people are part of the production system, and where leadership is a battle. When we move into the organic paradigm where people are potentials and heroes, where leadership is to be a role model and source of inspiration, and where curiosity and willingness to take risks are positive qualities, then analyses won't always work. Reid Hoffman, Co-Founder and Chairman of LinkedIn, says it the following way: "Welcome To Permanent Beta. We are all works in progress. Permanent Beta is a lifelong commitment to continuous personal growth. It is the mindset of every entrepreneur of life."[60]

Inspiration: The Leadership Perspective

Professor John Kotter from Harvard Business School puts it in the following way: The thought process behind management is Analyze –> Think –> Change, whereas the thought process behind leadership is See –> Feel –> Change. He also states that successful transformation is 70% leadership and 30% management.[61] Management is internally directed and involves getting things done on time, whereas leadership is externally directed: Creating the future. Sometimes these processes are compressed by sudden transformational events such as an act of terrorism, a natural catastrophe or individuals going through other life-changing experiences. Survivors from catastrophes tend to say the following: "I am different because of what I experienced".

Your challenge in your life is to identify and describe your dream. Henry David Thoreau wrote it this way: "Go confidently in the direction of your dreams – live the life you've imagined".[62] In a lighter vein, the lyrics of Oscar Hammerstein II in the 1949 musical *South Pacific* reflect the same life philosophy: "You gotta have a dream, if you don't have a dream, how you gonna have a dream come true?"

So, what is your dream?

I will now again invite you to some forced writing:

Forced Writing Exercise: Your Dream

Please take 6½ minutes to write down your dream. You must write without interruption. Associations will follow freely. If nothing else, then write your shopping list. Don't stop writing. You can always delete. Don't worry. You can do it. Now.

Flemming's Tale: Personal Journey

Flemming, while focusing on describing his Personal Journey, pinned down the following conclusions. He had now learned to steer – it was time to accelerate! His personal priorities were his wife and his close family. He loved art: Painting, sculpture, installation, opera, ballet, theater, music, and literature. He loved architecture: Cities and buildings. He loved skiing, fitness, and wellness. His potential for personal growth hinged on experiencing the world. He wanted to take calculated risks with a focus on wildness. He chose to reinvent himself with a rebellious touch. He decided to sense and enjoy every inch of potential adventure. And he focused on catalytic society – the creative interaction between government, civic society, and the corporate sector. In Flemming's tale you already sense an anticipation; a will to break free. Words like experiencing, wildness, rebellious, and adventure represent a strong urge for change – they are strong motivational drivers.

Jan's Tale: Personal Journey

Jan, while continuing his fruitful journey, became more and more aware of the difference between action and perception. He had always believed that if he did the right thing, then things would turn out right for him. However, in complex global matrix systems, this is seldom the case. Jan needed to focus more on the form of the message rather than the message itself. Form should not prevail over substance but his communication should be planned with the receiver's perspective in mind. It is not enough that the message is true; the receiver of the message also needs to *feel* that it is true. He became aware that he had a bad habit of neglecting eye contact when his inner dialogue took over. And since he was often in deep thoughts, this happened quite often. So he didn't need to change his approach to problem-solving, he simply needed to adapt his behavior, that is, the visible manifestation of his thinking. This simple change in habit did the trick and helped Jan appear professionally extrovert.

Key Learning

- Ask yourself: "In which life phase am I? And what's the next? And the next?"
- Prioritize talking with people and not at people.
- Define yourself based on normativity, authority, and integrity levels.
- Avoid compromising your ethical standards – not even when you're alone.
- Focus on the Why? instead of the What? and the How?
- Seek opportunities before anything else.
- Take responsibility for your mood and your behavior.
- Be thankful for what works.
- Create moments of joy.
- Give time for reflection.

6

How Do I Become Happy?

There is a crack in everything.
That's how the light comes in
Leonard Cohen

Every day above ground is a happy day. Think of your life as the result of your relationship management. You need to balance results and relationships to find happiness in business. At a certain point in life you may ask yourself: Is this what I want? Is my life meaningful? Am I happy? What is my personal life project? What is my desired goal in life? Is it a means or an objective?

As people, we need to have fulfilling relationships all the way round: Partner, children, parents, relatives, friends, bosses, peers, employees, and community – this is a mental model I call *Happiness 360*. I see these relationships as part of a gigantic Ferris[63] wheel. Imagine being at the center of the wheel that is your own life while navigating between these crucial groups of people:

Figure 12 Happiness 360

These can be grouped roughly as family, work, friends, and community:

- ⊗ **Family**: Partner, children, parents and relatives;
- ⊗ **Work**: Boss, peers and employees;
- ⊗ **Friends**; and
- ⊗ **Community.**

Friends and Community can originate from the most extraordinary places! Friends are usually people with whom you share experiences, interests and values; your community comprises a group that you identify with in some way, at some level. Community could include people from the area in which you live and the neighbors you greet, members of your sports club, it could be your church, it could also be a virtual community on Facebook or LinkedIn.

The model of the Ferris wheel is a cool tool that can be used to evaluate your perspective and balance in life. Your priorities will change during your life and you need to find out how these shifts will affect you and your closest. But it is also a compensatory model, if you only focus on a few stakeholders the wheel will not be in balance. The beauty of the concept is that an integrated personal effort will optimize your relationships all the way round and, not least, leave you feeling much better and energized.

A bonus advantage is that you may use this Happiness 360 model to optimize your network. When you are going to implement your Personal Business Plan you will need to go through your past and scrutinize it for relevant people that could be part of your future network. And you may as well start with kindergarten. Did you have any friends there who might come in handy now? What happened to your best friends from elementary school? Today it is extraordinarily easy to reconnect using social media and alumni portals. What about high school or college? There are hundreds of people whom you have known and whom you have lost contact with.

Now you may continue to *Family*. You may not have thought about how a cousin or a distant aunt or uncle may be able to help you carry your life ambition through, but you will be surprised how much potential help lures just around the corner. Next stop in the Happiness 360 model is *Work*, and therefore, Colleagues. Just think back on all the colleagues you have had. Some of them have come into influential positions and may be able to help you in your endeavor. Your principle should be: Why not? The worst thing that can happen is that you get a polite no, and then you're not worse off than before. Your community may also be a good source of network. Neighbors, former neighbors, co-workers from voluntary organizations, members of sports clubs; useful network originates from the most unsuspected places.

Everybody wants to be happy. A happy leader is a better leader. Happiness is contagious. Your approach to happiness can be as direct as your approach to budgeting. If you consciously work on improving your happiness you will become happier. It simply takes some discipline. One of the fundamental truths is that if you are not happy now, you will never be happy. Happiness happens in your head and will not miraculously materialize tomorrow. You need to find ways of reenergizing yourself in order to take care of yourself and your family. You can walk away from a plane crash; you can't walk away from your family.

Inspiration: Two Personal Stories

The first story deals with a COO who worked so much, that his eight year old son – after deliberation with his two younger siblings – pulled himself together and asked his mother: "Mom, can't we at least visit Dad?" The kids thought that their parents had divorced!

The second story describes a CEO,[64] who learned that he had only 100 days left to live. He writes in his diary, which was published posthumously, that the corporation, for which he worked, proudly informed their new associates that they wouldn't get to know their kids, but they would get to know their grand-children very well. For obvious reasons he no longer agreed with this prioritization.

You are happy when you obtain or achieve what you have agreed with yourself will make you happy. Happiness is the self-confidence to enjoy life, even under hard circumstances. In order to remain in control it is very often necessary to innovate and disrupt your habitual way of living. Albert Einstein said that problems cannot be solved using the same consciousness that created them. It is very difficult to stay alert, nimble and creative if you are trapped in the same environment, same context and same state of mind. So in order not to conform you need to reinvent yourself from time to time. In order to not simply continue to download past experiences, you need to look to the future for new ways of personal performance. You need to use lateral thinking, surprise others (including yourself) and have flexible fun.

I used to believe in the following paradigm:

Results ⟹ Relationships ⟹ Meaning ⟹ Happiness

Then, different audiences confronted me with the objection that this kind of linear thinking was simplistic – so I added a feedback loop:

Results ⟹ Relationships ⟹ Meaning ⟹ Happiness

However, for many people, this wasn't enough. And gradually, it dawned upon me, that I had been erroneous in my basic assumption. I implicitly believed that successful people became happy. Now I believe that happy people become successful! And this leads to the following model:

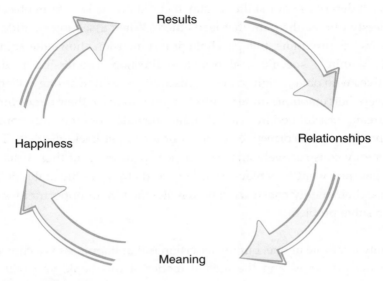

Figure 13 The Happiness Paradigm

An interesting dimension here is that I have gone from a linear perception to a circular perception. This perception much closer fits the perception of my wife. And, generally speaking, I have experienced this difference in perception as gender specific. Males tend to look at the world through a linear causal prism while females tend to look at life through a circular holistic prism. The secret of success in business and in life is being able to combine these two views – again a both/and solution. According to Indra Nooyi, Chairman and CEO of PepsiCo, the skill that is in shortest supply is the ability to re-conceptualize the business.[65] It takes strategic acuity to adapt and be both willing and able to think properly. You cannot think properly if you are sure you are right.

Many executives are better at describing their business model than at telling their own life story based on insight. Everybody has a story. Together, we will view your life story from each of the perspectives in the Happiness 360 model and focus on the relationships that will make you happy. Together, we will place your story in a wider context and extract relevant key lessons from the stories of others. We will answer your questions and clear the path for a happy future. It is not difficult – it simply takes some discipline. I will help you structure your questions. The answers are yours.

Discipline

Discipline is a fundamental personality trait which is closely correlated to success. It describes your ability to stay focused on the long term objective and relentlessly pursue the path that leads there. When assessing candidates with psychometric programs, this psychological dimension shows the ability to be flexible within a specific goal oriented direction. Leadership is direction. Executives who obtain high scores on discipline are often strong-willed people who keep their emotions under control in order to reach their target and realize their dream. Disciplined individuals might deviate from the path from time to time, but they take corrective action in order to get back on track. They use their energy constructively and have a clear perception of their value system and what they want to achieve. In other words they are life ambitious people who use their energy constructively to make the best of opportunities – rather than to solve problems.

I am only a sample of one, but my assertion is that happiness is a choice. If you follow the principles and the mental model of this book, you will become happier. Especially in the wake of a crisis, humanism and responsibility tends to take over from individualism and materialism.

Three Categories of Happiness

Martin Seligman, University of Pennsylvania psychologist and director of the Positive Psychology Network, defines three categories of happiness:[66]
  "The pleasant life"
  "The good life"
  "The meaningful life"

1. The pleasant life
This is the Hollywood happiness – smiling, feeling good, and being ebullient – but the problem with it is that not everybody can achieve it. And that is a matter of genetic predisposition; perhaps half of us have it, which means the other half will never get to feel ecstatic. Brains are simply created differently. The impulse for feelings lies in the *amygdala*, a small area the size of a walnut deeply imbedded in the brain. The amygdala plays a significant role in the

creation of feeling, especially fear and worry, and it is amygdala that sends the first impulse about feeling activity.

The signal is transmitted to the frontal lobes of the brain where it is coordinated with the information from other parts of the brain. People who primarily show activity in the right frontal lobe often experience negative feelings such as anger, fear, and worry. People with high activity in the left frontal lobe more often experience positive feelings such as optimism and enthusiasm. The right frontal lobe is thus the center for negative feelings and the left the center for positive feelings. By consistently complimenting your colleagues or children (or even your dog) you actually increase your own joy.[67]

2. The good life

This rests on knowing what your strengths are and then re-crafting your life to use them – in work, in love, friendship, leisure, and parenting. It is about being absorbed, immersed, at one with the music. The psychologist Mihaly Csikszentmihalyi (pronounced "cheeks-sent-me-high") from the University of Chicago launched the flow concept.[68] Flow is a feeling of total presence that you can achieve when you are totally immersed in an activity which is the epitome of its own purpose. Flow therefore occurs when we direct all of our attention towards the execution of a specific project and disregard everything else – including the purpose. We only become happy when we immerse ourselves in what we are really good at and what we love.

3. The meaningful life

This is about identifying your signature strengths and then using them in the service of something you believe is bigger than you are. You do not have to be conventionally happy to achieve this form of happiness. Winston Churchill and Abraham Lincoln were two profound depressives who dealt with their condition by leading good and meaningful lives.[69] Churchill, who has been named the greatest orator of all times, succeeded against all odds. He was depressive, he stammered, he was a heavy drinker and, in his memoirs, he reveals that he never held a public speech without rehearsing it eight times.[70]

Circumstances do not always determine emotional states. Seligman acknowledges that extreme poverty is a downer, but says, "Once you're above the safety net, people in wealthier nations are not by and large noticeably happier than those in poorer nations." Climate is not a crucial factor. Nor is money: "If you look at lottery winners, they get happy for a few months. But a year later, they're back where they were."

Many of the things that we crave will not really affect our state of happiness. The grass is not always greener on the other side of the fence. Even a catastrophe – say, being diagnosed with cancer – does little to alter one's overall outlook. "On average," Seligman observes, "people with a life-threatening disease are not necessarily unhappier than the rest of the population. Of course, a cascade of bad things happening can make a difference. But if you have one really bad thing, generally you're not unhappier". The two conditions that may matter most are marital status and religious belief, Seligman says. "Married people are happier than any other configuration of people. And religious people are usually happier than nonreligious people."[71]

Despite Jean-Paul Sartre's famous "Hell is other people" most people actually feel happier when they are with others. And since married people are presumed to be less alone than singles and that many religions and churches involve a strong community aspect, it could well be that togetherness is the key to happiness. This, at least, seems to be the most fundamental finding from the science of happiness.[72]

So, love the ones you are with. Spoil your partner, cherish your loved ones. Goodwill in family relationships is like money in the bank. Family is existential. Families forgive each other. Families work around problems. Families require effort and patience. They are your family; you cannot just throw them out on the street. The trust you build at home is the most important trust of all.

Throughout your life you need to create the trust and the coexistence that will result in continued reciprocity and generosity. The interest in success has never been greater – if you Google the word "success" you get more than 1 billion hits. Success in business presupposes success on the personal level. Your hinterland needs to be in order if you are to continually deliver excellent results. This means that you need to have the courage to commit yourself to your family – the courage to be a whole person. If not, the consequence will probably be a life crisis where you feel groggy and burnt out.

Dan Baker, a psychologist who directs the Life Enhancement Program at Canyon Ranch in Tucson, Arizona, supervised a survey of the mental health canon. His team found 54 000 studies on depression and only 415 – less than 1% – on happiness. So, according to these studies, what makes us happy? "It is the ability to practise appreciation or love,"'" says Baker. "That sounds sappy, but studies show that when people engage in appreciative activity, they are using more neo-cortical, prefrontal functions – higher-level brain functions".[73] There you go, skeptics: Happiness is an exercise for smart people. So, is the glass half-empty, half-full or, as the engineers say, twice as big as it needs to be? Happiness may consist in recognizing that we cannot always be happy; that ambitions are worth fighting for but not dying for; that a sense of humour, even of the absurd, is necessary for a lifesaving sense of proportion. In business, two of the most important qualities that help us to keep events in perspective are humor and humility.

What is My Challenge?

Before reading further you must realize what your issues are. You must carefully chart your actual situation. Is your focus more directed towards business challenges or towards personal challenges? Where do you want to make changes in order to improve your state of mind and feeling of happiness?

Happiness may be defined as experience divided by expectation:

$$\text{HAPPINESS} = \frac{\text{EXPERIENCE}}{\text{EXPECTATION}}$$

If you have high expectations, the outcome of any activity or project must be highly rewarding in order to meet these expectations. However, if your expectations are lower the experience does not need to be as exhilarating before you achieve a feeling of happiness. The ideal is to be able to set ambitious targets and then reach them! A career is built on a focused effort. If you know the target, you become the target. The personal challenge and reward lies in thriving while you make the effort.

Inspiration: The Happiness Formula

Life coach Pete Cohen believes that the simple key to a happy life is to occasionally take time off from work, exercise regularly and make an effort in your relationship. He continues and suggests the following specific formula for happiness with ratings from one to ten on each criterion giving a total maximum of 100[74]

Happiness = Personal Characteristics + Existence Needs
+ Higher Order Needs

$$Happiness = P + 5E + 3H$$

P is the value of the combination of two questions:

1. On *personal characteristics* and traits: "To what extent do you see yourself as someone who is outgoing, energetic, flexible, and open to change?"
2. On your *outlook on life*: "To what extent do you see yourself as someone who takes a positive outlook on life, bounces back quickly from setbacks, feels that you, and not fate, is driving your life?"

E is the value assigned to a third question:

3. On basic *existence needs*: "To what extent do you feel your basic needs in life are met in relation to personal health, financial subsistence, personal safety, freedom of choice, sense of belonging, and access to knowledge?"

H is the value assigned to the final question:

4. About *higher order* happiness needs: "To what extent are you currently able to call on support of people close to you, immerse yourself in what you are doing, meet your expectations, engage in meaningful activities that give you a sense of purpose, feel a clear sense of who you are, and what you are about?"

If you, for example, answer 8 on question 1 and 7 on question 2, P equals 15. If you answer 7 on question 3, 5E equals 35. If you then answer 8 on question 4, 3H equals 24. Your total happiness score is thus 15 + 35 + 24 = 74 out of 100.

Adaptation

Research conducted by the psychologist Edward Diener from the University of Illinois has shown that as we become wealthier, we adjust our expectations. What we aspired to yesterday becomes today's new baseline.[75] This would imply that following monetary life strategies creates less happiness than following relationship-based life strategies does. Ambition is so strong a human driver that no matter how much you earn and acquire, you will never be satisfied. You also need to be fully aware of who it is you are trying to please. Is it your parents, your partner, your neighbor, your bosses, your employees, or yourself?

Research by David Lykken from the University of Michigan has shown that just as we appear to overemphasize the perceived long-term benefit of, for example, winning the lottery we also tend to believe that sudden, dramatic negative events (for example loss of mobility, sight, or hearing) will have a lasting impact on our overall happiness.[76] Research consistently shows that people who have experienced some traumatic event, whilst experiencing a short-term drop in wellbeing, soon return to near normal levels of happiness. Psychologists call this adjustment to new circumstances *adaptation*. Based on research of 4000 twins David Lykken concluded that 50% of one's satisfaction with life stems from genetic programming. This finding has led to the idea that each of us has a predetermined happiness level. No matter what happens in our life we tend to return to our set range within a short period of time.

However, according to research by Edward Diener, there are two life events that seem to affect the happiness of people permanently: Loss of a spouse and loss of a job. It may take five to eight years for a widow or widower to regain her or his previous sense of wellbeing.[77] One of my clients, who had lost his wife, explained to me that his sorrow was like a background computer program running permanently, slowing down his whole system. I have talked to thousands of executives who have lost their jobs and often the effect is like a depth charge where you only see the shock waves after a certain period of time has elapsed. I usually compare the situation to that of a malfunctioning radar system. Signals are not detected and navigation is incomplete. At the same time, however, the unemployed executive typically tends to act as if he or she is in full control of the situation.

If you want to thrive, the core challenge is to manage expectations – both in relation to yourself and in relation to others. We need to be both ambitious and realistic. Objects are empty. We give meaning to them and fill them through our actions and our positions. Therefore it is possible to push the barriers and extend the limits by thinking "Wouldn't it be wonderful, if . . ." or "Think what I could achieve, if . . ." One of my clients once said to me: "In my family the men live to be 90. And I'm only 45. So I have half of my life and two thirds of my working life in front of me". To me that signals a fundamental attitude of counting up and not down. Although our marital status and the number of children we have may affect the priority we assign to certain leisure activities, time spent with friends and family is seen as a vital support that can provide that important feeling of togetherness and belonging. It represents a regenerative activity that makes you more stress resistant in the long run.

Perhaps the most intangible key to happiness is not to get what you want but to want what you get. Let me illustrate this by the concept of "happy marriage". Many researchers have tried to determine the characteristics of a happy marriage. Most often this has been done by trying to identify common traits between the two partners. Many anticipated explanatory variables have been studied: Income, age, education, tolerance, patience, and so on – all without any significant result. It has not been possible to establish a clear correlation between mutual resemblance and happiness. One study, however, from the *Journal of Experimental Social Psychology* shows that the defining characteristic of a happy marriage is that the husband consistently ranks the wife higher than she ranks herself and vice versa.[78] This determined positive perspective seems to color the entire relationship. Placing the respective partner on a pedestal and maintaining his or her place there guarantees a happy marriage. This could be characterized as naïvety by observers, but if it secures your marriage and makes both of you happy, so what? I placed my wife on a pedestal more than 30 years ago, and she has never left it!

I am not recommending a naïve life attitude. We are not talking about glossy pictures that could have been taken from a lifestyle magazine, rather about being fully aware of positive and negative messages and events. Ambrose Bierce, an American journalist and satirist, described the future as that period of time in which our affairs prosper, our friends are true, and our happiness is assured.[79]

Dopamine

The Danish philosopher Tor Norretranders has considered happiness from both a philosophical and a physiological point of view. He concludes with a very simple happiness equation:[80]

Joy × Control < 1

The factors in the equation are complementary, so that:

- More Joy leads to less Control
- Total Control leads to no Joy
- Total loss of Control does not lead to total Joy!

There appears to be an imbalance and, in order to fully understand this, we need to delve into a substance called dopamine and a phenomenon called *Reward Prediction Error*. A team of psychologists, Alice M. Isen from Cornell University, and And U. Turken and F. Gregory Ashby from University of California, proposed that a messenger substance in the brain called dopamine was related to feelings of reward and motivation.[81] Professor of Neuroscience Wolfram Schultz from Cambridge University, studied the role of dopamine in the early 1990s.[82] The research led to a groundbreaking discovery, namely that dopamine is released not upon reward itself but upon expectation of reward. Dopamine is released when the cell receives the message that the organism has experienced a positive result that is more than we expected. Thus, when we expect a good thing, no dopamine is pumped out. This leads to an unending quest for something that we can only obtain when we are not sure that we will get it! The sequence described above meshes perfectly with the concept of adaptation. It also provides a powerful rationale for substance abuse. Cocaine prevents the disappearance of dopamine and thereby prolongs a feeling of joy. Alcohol and nicotine stimulate the release of dopamine and create a feeling of joy. In many cases this state of "joy" is followed by signs of depression when the cells once again and inevitably become deprived of dopamine.

What can we learn from this? Let go of the need to control: Loosen the grip on the ego. Lead from the future as it emerges. There is always a team behind a successful leader. That is why, when hiring, you need to focus on people whose egos come last and whose desire to work collaboratively comes first. Remember the Golden Rule of Team-Working: Contribute with more than your share. In a team consisting of six people each and every team member must contribute with at least one fifth! This principle is also valid in families.

Why Must I Do Something Now?

There is a reason why you have this book in your hands. You may be experiencing some frustration or lacking some satisfaction in your daily life. What would you define as your burning platform? Why can you simply not let things go on as they are for one more year? There is no reason to accept unhappiness. A student once asked a psychology professor teaching a course on Motivation:

"How do you motivate yourself to stop smoking?" The answer was: "You simply stop". By mobilizing your subconscious, you will be able to register and observe the mechanisms behind your potentially destructive behavior and start focusing on the positives in life. What would it be like to be fully open to the possibilities that are emerging, regardless of their threat to habit, comfort, and stereotyped expectations?

Inspiration: The Impasse Perspective

In his book *Getting Unstuck: How Dead Ends Become New Paths*, Dr Timothy Butler, Senior Fellow and Director of Career Development Programs at Harvard Business School, writes that,

> the meaning of an impasse, although first expressed as a failure or in an internalized notion of inadequacy, is a request for us to change our way of thinking about ourselves and our place in the world. Impasse is a psychological process, outside of time and space. At impasse our model – our cognitive map of life and of the way we're going to fit into it – is no longer working. We all carry a representation of the world, our work, how we do our work, and how we fit in and where we're going; and that map is always inadequate in a number of ways. The norm is change. We need to change our repertoire of ways in which we approach life challenges.[83]

The symptoms of impasse may be many. One of the most common symptoms is usually referred to as *stress*. I regularly meet stressed people – many of them highly successful. Stress and success seem to be two sides of the same coin. When I ask them what their symptoms are, most respond by mentioning physical symptoms. On this basis I have developed the following traffic light:

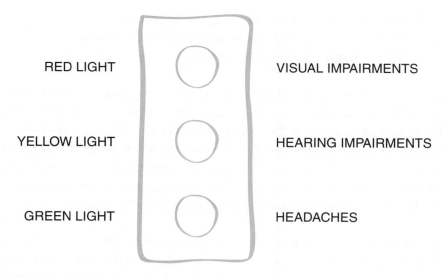

Figure 14 The Traffic Light

The principle is that headaches are not dangerous. They are not productive and not nice to have, but occasional headaches are not critical, so it is considered a green light. If the pressure continues, you might experience popping in your ears and reduced hearing. This is annoying and represents a yellow light. If, however, pressure keeps mounting and you start seeing spots in front of your eyes or having difficulties focusing, then it is a red light and you should stop doing whatever you are doing. This might include altering your perspective on the behavior you want to change. Sometimes the most appropriate way out is action. This means stop making lists about the things you need to do and start performing the tasks in real time. It is extremely stressful to do something other than what you know is most urgent or most important. A Spanish proverb describes it this way: *Tomorrow is often the busiest day of the week.* The level of stress increases when you run in vain, not when you run fast. Another change of behavior could be to smile and act happy instead of being irritated and frustrated by the multiple tasks ahead.

When you operate at the boundary of your maximum performance level you operate at a short fuse – your inclusiveness and flexibility go down the drain. The state of being on constant standby takes its toll on you. Whereas some level of stress can be positive, unaddressed stress is negative and may, if prolonged, lead to galvanization – meaning that you become emotionally callous. There are three good reasons to address stress:

1. In order to protect your health and your appearance.
2. In order to maintain a good relationship with your closest.
3. In order to become better at your work.

The opposite of stress is not relaxation but overview. As long as you act – rather than constantly reacting – you will not go down with stress. One of the consequences of today's stress and insecurity is cocooning. When confronted with too much complex information, the world seems threatening; one instinctive reaction to this is to retreat into a known and comfortable environment, which is often the family. Therefore we observe cocooning – a trend towards presence and intimacy as a reaction against superficiality and alienation.

When observing and working with executives I often get an impression of tremendous haste. It seems as if we are all caught in a kind of Bermuda triangle between meetings, messages and mobility. In addition to face-to-face meetings, our mobile office communication interfaces today include e-mails, cellphone messages, social networks and video conferencing. We are constantly "on call" and always accessible to the requests, queries, and demands of others.

Inspiration: The Stress Perspective

We talk a great deal about stress nowadays but I do not think it is because people have become more fragile, rather because sometimes we all want too much at the same time. We expect the perfect life. We want a stellar career at 26, true love at 28, a magnificent house and two kids at 30. This is not a daydream, it is actually a requirement and "Because we're worth it" is our motto. This may lead to deep and brutal life stress because in all that really matters, it is life that decides. Although they don't make it any better, the great stress we now experience does not stem from smartphones or e-mails, it comes from something far bigger: Unrealistic expectations in life. If we want to lower our stress level, this might on the surface seem to be about taking one more week's holiday or learning to turn off the smartphone – but if you look deeper, it is about looking life, as it is, in the eye.

The important message here is change. If you feel miserable then you have to change your behavior – nothing less will suffice. You have to act upon the pattern of dissatisfaction that you can identify. There is no alternative to a new attitude. Nobody else will make you happy – you are the only one who can do it! You can choose to start mornings by giving yourself a high-five in the mirror. You can also choose to brush your teeth using the other hand in order to provoke some physical change processes in your brain. For now the most important thing to remember is: "I have got to change". I once worked with a CFO, who stammered. He was systematically interrupted after a few sentences, when he paused. Together, we trained him to say the first sentences without pausing, and the result was amazing. The simple fact of concentrating on a flow of meaning gave him unprecedented power in the executive group.

Inspiration: The Human Brain

The human brain is the hungriest organ in the body. Even though it only counts for 2.5% of total body weight, it greedily consumes 20% of the body's oxygen uptake. As the brain can't store energy, blood flows constantly and produces enough electrical energy to light up a 10 watt light bulb. No wonder that you might get brain pain when you concentrate deeply for long periods of time. Actually, since the brain is not a muscle, the pain is not located there, it just feels that way.[84]

When looking at the evolution of the human brain, we can identify three stages: The reptile brain, the limbic system, and the logical brain. The three of them are still present in the brains of today's human beings. The reptile brain assists in four key areas: eating, reproduction, fight, and flight. The limbic system is where feelings, relationships, recognition, and motivation reside. The logical brain is the computer that tries to keep control. Early in their careers many ambitious executives rely too heavily on the rational dimension of a specific leadership issue. More seasoned professionals know that considering the emotional dimension adds to the quality of the solution and gives a more sustainable long-term result. How can it be that we, as individuals, are so intelligent and, yet, in groups so hopeless? The explanation is that many of us are illiterates in the emotional area.

Even when it is documented that something is true, it is not accepted as a fact before we feel that it is true. Despite all we learn, we do not feel that something is true before the limbic system, which is placed in the middle of the brain and which handles our emotions, tells us that it is true. When we are stressed or worried our possibilities to influence our surroundings are decreased, but when we are relaxed and optimistic our capabilities are markedly improved. The pace of life hasn't changed, even if the pace of communication has. People still fall in love at the same pace and they still trust each other at the same pace.

How Can I Obtain 20/20 Vision?

In order to help you visualize a challenging personal goal and clarify your ambition level, I will ask you to do the following exercise. Please focus on your learning curve for the last 20 years. There is no doubt that you have become a much more knowledgeable person in that time – both from a personal and from a professional point of view. Try to identify the events or actions that triggered the most learning and personal growth. Are there any commonalities between these events or actions? What is the pattern in your learning behavior? When and why did you grow most? Please keep in mind that Learning is closely correlated to Wellbeing, meaning that the more you learn, the better you feel.

When you have finished this exercise I will ask you to set yourself a new challenge. You have experienced a steep learning curve for the last 20 years. This learning may be symbolized by the shaded area under the curve. Remember integration from the math course in high school? If you look at this shaded area

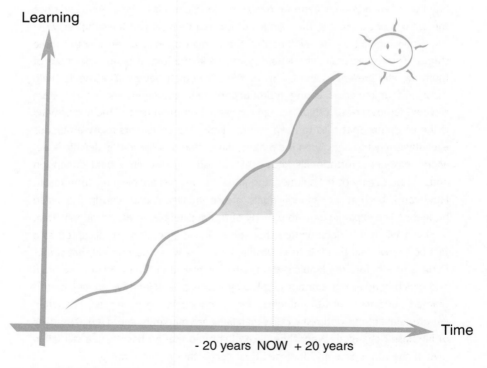

Figure 15 The 20/20 Vision

for the last 20 years your challenge is to ensure that the shaded area under the curve for the next 20 years is at least as big. This means that you should aim at learning and growing just as much or more in the next 20 years as you have learnt and grown for the last 20 years. Your new target is your 20/20 vision. So what goals can you possibly invent that are challenging enough to live up to this tough demand? You will probably have to look in totally new directions in order to expand your own interests and horizon. And then after 20 years if you are, for example, approaching retirement, demographics tell us that you will probably have 20 more active years when you have to challenge yourself even more just to stay abreast of societal and technological changes. Experience tells us that, if you don't have a purpose when you retire, you die! So what could you possibly do that would surprise both yourself and your surroundings?

Inspiration: First-Loop and Second-Loop Learning

You can also use the 20/20 vision figure in another way. You may distinguish between first-loop learning and second-loop learning.

First-loop learning is what you actually experience and learn. Second-loop learning is contextualizing and communicating what you have learned to others. These two processes are inherently different. First-loop learning occurs inside your own value system – you intuitively agree with your own observations and judgments. If you sit alone in your study on your home turf, it is easy to agree with yourself. When you then have to present your ideas and confront the value systems of others, the ideas suddenly seem less bright and less convincing. You then have to take all the necessary feedback and integrate it in your first construct. This is second-loop learning. If, for example, you are writing a report, the challenge is to front-load all your knowledge so it is presented on the first pages in order to establish a common frame of reference. This creation of a common platform will ease the comprehension process and contribute significantly to the quality of the communication process. It's always about consistently taking the perspective of the receiver.

When you experience something new you become energized. It is important to manage that energy and focus on the longer term, on what it will take to be great. This corresponds to the long-term principle formulated by Stephen R. Covey: "Begin with the end in mind". If you have difficulties making a choice, apply the 10-Year Rule: "10 years from now, what will I be glad I did?"[85]

In order to help you prioritize your future actions I have compiled a list of suggestions for a happier life. Some of the suggestions will resonate with you while others may seem irrelevant. Select the ones that are most meaningful to you and make them operational by adding specific action points to each of them. Do not forget to put in a realistic time frame and a deadline.

Table 6 Suggestions for a Happier Life

Maintain balance in your life.
Put effort into close relationships.
Meet new people and break out of established patterns.
Immerse yourself in the moment.
Exercise and rest.
Put up stretch targets for yourself – Big Hairy Ambitious Goals.
Be brave – research shows that people more often regret what they didn't do than what they did.
Be your own "Yes" person.
Meditate – it may help you combat stress.
Be positive about yourself.
Remember to enjoy the journey.
Be aware of your energy source.
Express and show gratitude.
Visualize the future that you dream of.
Enjoy life with all senses.
Learn to forgive.
Write a diary.
Buy experiences – not things.
Define who you are and not what you are.
Reward yourself for each milestone, think of all the good things coming out of reaching your target.
Find a partner – in business and/or in life.
Try something new – break your habits.
Be a good parent.
Define your preferred role in your family, among your friends and in your network.
Make a successful plan: Write it down, tell others about it and act upon it.

Usain Bolt, the 100m and 200m world champion, exemplifies this by putting up a stretch target when, after breaking the world record and becoming the fastest man on Earth, he then declared that his next ambition was to become a legend. When President John F. Kennedy in 1961 declared his ambition to put a man on the moon before the end of the decade, it sounded unrealistic in the ears of many. But this ambitious goal became the symbol of the dynamism that was created in many parts and at many levels of American society.

Flemming's Tale: Happiness 360

Flemming had come up with some challenging insights. He fully understood that when leaving Realdania, he would no longer be the CEO of a mega success, he would only be Flemming. He also discovered that it was all about daring, that he was energized by flow and change. He realized that he would no longer have the entire organization to service him. He needed to focus on developing himself – if not, it all stopped. He decided to trust his intuition to an even higher degree. Furthermore he chose to build his future by accepting global board roles. He also chose to join innovative think tanks. Flemming also built his 20/20 vision – he painted a clear picture of where he wanted to be in 20 years. And finally he experienced a deep attraction to and obligation towards living up to the name given to him by a Chinese partner 博思明 *Bo Si Ming* (meaning Profound Bright Thinking).

Jan's Tale: A Life Well-Lived

Jan Asmussen defined his central challenge as morphing from specialist to businessman. He strongly felt a need to document all his decisions which were not a part of his job description. Since he had a well-developed service gene, he instinctively and loyally took upon him orphan tasks, both CFO tasks and other tasks not taken by anybody else. This made Jan perform a whole amount of invisible work for which he got no credit. He needed to become more visible by continually training at CFO tasks and also become affiliated to a CFO network. Due to his solid performance and high Engagement Survey results he had been attached to a mentor program, which also gave him general management experience. His take on happiness was quite charming. He described it as *A Life Well Lived*: A successful father, a successful businessman and an adventurer, that is, an enjoyer of life. He wanted to be seen as a leader both capable of delegating and executing and especially behave as a person with exceptional integrity – manifesting his inner potential to the outer world.

Key Learning

- Take a tour in the Happiness 360 wheel and visualize your position in life right now.
- Focus on the relationships that will make you happy.
- Build trust at home and at work.
- Use humor and humility to keep events in perspective.
- Count up and not down in life – it's a mindset.
- Place your partner on a pedestal.
- Let go of the need to control – loosen the grip on your ego.
- Change your behavior if you feel miserable.
- Aim at learning more the next 20 years than you have learned the last 20 years.
- Apply the 10-Year Rule: "10 years from now, what will I be glad I did?"

7

How Do I Reinvent Myself?

" There are no traffic jams along the extra mile *"*
Roger Staubach

What do executive search consultants look for in a candidate? Until 10 years ago, the answer was very simple: Results, results, and results. Past performance was considered to be the best predictor of future performance. No matter what, business is about creating results; they may be growth rates, market share gains, free cash flow or other key performance indicators. The foundation for a successful career is tangible or hardcore results and your reputation is the sum of your past performance. There's no elevator to success – you have to take the stairs. In addition to that you may have excellent leadership and interpersonal competencies. At the end of the day you are measured by the value you create for your organization and your future career will depend on the potential value you will create for your new organization. But nowadays, there is more to the story than just performance and results.

I have already touched on the fundamental concept of *Learning Agility* which we will now explore in detail. The construct of Learning Agility consists of five dimensions:

1. Mental Agility
2. People Agility
3. Change Agility
4. Results Agility
5. Self-Awareness.

Mental agility – ability to examine problems in unique and unusual ways

People agility – skilled communicator who can work with diverse types of people

Change agility – likes to experiment and comfortable with change

Results agility – delivers results in challenging first-time situations

Self-Awareness – extent to which an individual knows his or her true strengths and weaknesses

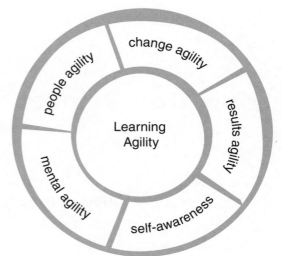

Figure 16 Five Factors In Learning Agility
Source: Kenneth P. De Meuse, What's Smarter than IQ? (Korn/Ferry Institute, October 2011)

Learning Agility is not correlated with age, gender, education, or other demographics – yet only 15% of the population is learning agile. It is a psychographic, not a demographic. However, there is evidence that Learning Agility increases with experience and career trajectory. People with low Learning Agility tend to focus on the destination whereas people with high Learning Agility focus on the journey.

The typical picture of a career person is that Results Agility ranks highest, followed by Mental Agility and People Agility. Most often the lowest score is Change Agility.[86] What is needed to cope with change is mental plasticity and most of us are more or less content within the mold that formed us. Mental Agility is a broader concept than Intelligence. Sometimes too much intellectual horsepower looks like arrogance. Mentally agile people are able to connect the dots; they look for patterns and root causes, and can explain their thinking. An interesting finding is that the Results dimension includes the leadership behavior most often associated with charisma and ability to show the way. So in all fairness your results include the leadership leverage that you perform through other people. Creating results is about making a positive impact on the behavior of others.[87] I do not believe in the old adage: "People are our most important asset". As Jim Collins points out: "The right people are our most important asset"[88] and the right people are those who produce results.

Reaching the top of a corporation requires ambition and hard work. It is a question of control as well as being able to cope with the long haul. In the process you will inevitably make some enemies but critique has a tendency to mute when the results speak for themselves. Practice makes perfect and through inexorable work discipline you can practice and become good at what you choose to focus on. Diligence and results are the best branding for any ambitious executive. Furthermore, successful leaders often dare to take the road less travelled and are willing to submit themselves, their situation, and their position to constant and various challenges.

Diversity is the precondition for creativity. In order to activate your creativity it is important to let yourself be provoked, challenged, and inspired by new contrasts. Next time you put on a jacket, try putting the other arm in the sleeve first. Your brain will start looking for a program that is simply not there. The energy that comes from breaking habits can be used to focus even more on your strengths and identify even more opportunities.

The business challenge is to be able to look beyond traditional industry classifications and systematically combine the key competencies of the corporation with creativity in order to gain new customers. I'd like you to try the following short exercise:

Forced Writing Exercise: Key Competencies

Take 6½ minutes and write down one or two great opportunities that lie ahead for your organization. Then write down one or two great problems that your customers have. Don't stop writing. Lastly name one or two areas in which your corporation's competitors have an offer which the customers evaluate as better.

As soon as you can verbalize these issues, the concept of key competency starts making more sense.

What characterizes great organizations is their ability to reconcile contradictions: Centralization and decentralization, globalization and individualization, rationalization and growth, profit and investment, consolidation and development, planning and implementation, as well as technology and emotions. These contradicting tendencies are to be found in the same organization at different evolutionary stages and they alternate over time. The successful top executive is able to span the different leadership styles needed in each phase and this presupposes a broad bandwidth. The ever-increasing need in our globalized business world for understanding different cultures demands, in itself, a breadth in bandwidth as opposed to self-centering.

Exercise: The STAR Approach

This is a very useful interview technique that was developed using competency-based interview questioning. It can also be used by you to illustrate your successful career.

STAR stands for:

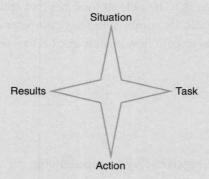

This simple technique possesses all the qualities of a professional tool: It is simple, it is effective and it follows our natural way of structuring communication. It will help you develop convincing cases that will be very handy as documentation of your proven leadership skills. The line of questioning covers many different competencies, for example, Creativity, Political Flair, Leadership, Communication, Determination, Resilience, and Analytical Skills. The questions could go like this:

Creativity: Describe a situation where traditional solutions or methods did not work? What was your task? What did you do? And what was the result? In which areas of your present job is it possible to show creativity and renewal?

Political Flair: Tell me about a situation where you carried out a task in which many different interests were at stake? What was the conflict about? What did you do? What was the result?

Leadership: What is the toughest leadership decision you have had to make? What was your task? What was your line of action? What was the result? How was the decision accepted?

Communication: Tell me about a situation where you formulated a vision for your area of responsibility? How did you communicate it? What did you do to prepare yourself? What were the results?

Determination: Give me an example of a decision that you made extremely quickly? Why was it necessary to act based on incomplete information? What was the consequence? What did you learn?

Resilience: What is the most stressful work situation you have found yourself in? How did you get through it? How is the present situation? What have you learned?

Analytical Skills: What is the biggest and most complex problem you have faced in the last six months? What was your task? What did you do? What was the result?

Use the Appendix and *The Personal Business Plan* from thepersonalbusinessplan. com and update it with ten STAR examples. It will give you a slice of life and these examples will come in real handy in all situations where you need to document your results. As you can no doubt see, this line of questioning gives you a great opportunity to paint a realistic picture of your accomplishments. You can prepare mini-cases, which will emphasize the competencies that you want to project. As listeners we tend to believe our own deductions more than the messages which are explicitly directed towards us, so you do not have to say that you are conscientious if the mini-cases clearly demonstrate it. You don't have to tell an interviewer that you are resilient if the mini-cases show beyond doubt that you are tough.

The important point about competencies is that they are personal. They are your competencies and they follow you into your new job. Executive search consultants look for what you bring to the table, not your boss, not your employees, not your department, not your division, and not your corporation. It is about you. And the better you are at presenting yourself through small stories about yourself, the clearer the picture of you that emerges.

The world of sport provides convincing illustrations of what we are up against when we seek to be among the best globally. At the Winter Olympic Games in Vancouver in 2010 the difference between gold medal and no medal was often under 2%. In the four-man bobsleigh the difference was less than 0.2%! The sports world is not that different from the world of business; often only extremely narrow margins represent the difference between success and the rest!

Whatever the result, if you are unable to measure it, it doesn't count. In my business we document everything. If it is not registered in our database, it doesn't exist and it didn't happen. However, we always remember to combine the result with the quality of the process. Quality is the relation between subject and object – and you are an essential part of that equation. When you concentrate you will realize your own effect on your surroundings. The more mature you become the more interested you become in the effect of your actions and communication on other people rather than focusing on what they think of you. When using your intuition freely (Claus Otto Scharmer calls it *presencing*) you see yourself as part of the total picture. You are able to observe yourself while fully being in the process – you may experience it as a third-eye perspective. A pivotal dimension here is quality consciousness, a consciousness which benefits both the quality of your life and the quality of your work. In reality the challenge is to be present in the here and now while consistently looking forward to and enjoying the onward journey. The only place you have ever met other people is in the now.

> *"* In attention lies the cure.
> That to which you give attention grows. *"*
> *Unknown*

We live in a society of information overflow; a world of abundance where the scarcest resource is human attention. The average attention span of an adult is three minutes. Therefore you need to focus and prioritize. One of the secrets behind *The Personal Business Plan* is that it makes your Life Ambition explicit. Your subconscious soon starts to filter all the information that is presented to you. You will start looking at the world through a lens, which is your own best future. So what do you want for yourself as a brand? That which you believe in, works. Believe in something. So what constitutes good quality in your life? Answer this question and you will be set for the pole position.

What am I Willing to Sacrifice?

Consider early on in your career whether or not you really want to be a top executive. And if you do, then why do you want it?

AESC again points out a few relevant questions concerning your desire to make it to the top:[89]

- Do you truly enjoy a leadership role?
- Do you have a yearning to be in control and manage others, or would you rather work on your own?
- Do you enjoy (or at least respond well to) the pressures of organizational responsibility and accountability?

The pressure brought about by positive expectations contributes in itself to creating results and leadership is, to a large extent, about stubbornly keeping a positive outlook. While positive, a top executive must not be gullible. As the French former businessman and politician Bernard Tapie says: "It takes two gentlemen to make a gentleman's agreement". All experiences should be angled positively and all opportunities should be fully exploited. Focus needs to be on the potential for success and not on the fear of fiasco.

Some people have a more positive disposition than others – a good basic mood. Typically it requires great self-confidence to dare to believe in the future and to focus on one's own towering strengths, and the organization's key competencies. It is not enough to be satisfied with the status quo – you need to inspire those around you to change, and praise your colleagues and employees when they create good results. The successful top executive is characterized by optimism, stamina, and robustness; this combination of qualities forms the precondition for general satisfaction and belief in the future. Optimism is a life choice.

Relationship Robustness

We have moved from a concept of work-life balance over a concept of work-life integration to a concept of work-life navigation. You need a career compass to steer you through your work-life. Actually, I have never understood the dichotomy between life and work. To me work is a part of life and cannot be seen as separate from it. With the accelerating development of real-time communication technology it would be futile to even try to maintain a sharp distinction between work and free time. Which reminds me of a cartoon, I saw: Two businessmen in black suits standing on the sidewalk talking to each other. One says to the other: "I'm working on my work/work balance."

When even Madonna points out that "You should never make work the main project of your life" then we have certainly come far! However much we may enjoy our work, most of us work to live and do not live to work.

If it makes your life easier, you might want to look at your family as internal customers. How would a customer satisfaction analysis look if the respondents were your family? Would your child rate you as an excellent listener or parent? Would your partner positively evaluate your presence? Throughout your business and personal life it is important to create the collaborative trust and the teamwork that leads to reciprocity and generosity. Remember that transparency is a two-way street and that leadership is about reducing uncertainty – it requires a new kind of openness. When you obtain sufficient self-awareness, you obtain sufficient robustness in your relationships. Natural leadership presupposes a generosity of spirit and a readiness to trust people.

> " The more people trust you, the more they buy from you.
> If your service is too generous, your clients will love you,
> but you will go broke. "
> *David Ogilvy*

In *Making a Life, Making a Living: Reclaiming Your Purpose and Passion in Business and in Life*, Mark Albion recounts the stories of a dozen fast-trackers who started over, choosing to dedicate their passion to a better self . . . and a better world.[90] If your career has lost its meaning, this book may help you find the courage to start over and motivate you to reach for your dreams and grab them. When you are back on the right track, your feeling will be one of "I cannot not do this!"

Work provides money, recognition, and content. Content is like flesh on the bones. All three elements are important in a balanced life. I also tend to look at work as consisting of opportunity (can), duty (must), and pleasure (will). A mix of these three variables is always present in a job. Bruce Dickinson, the lead singer of Iron Maiden and former pilot for a charter airline company, was once asked why he worked as a pilot. Was it because of the money? His answer was "If it was only for the money, I didn't need to sing in Iron Maiden, either".

Some people just do things because they are fun and challenging, and offer valuable relationships and experiences.

Time has significant signal value; just like salary, it signifies both recognition and reward. When you choose to spend time with somebody you attribute value to that person. When you pay a salary you indirectly express satisfaction with services rendered. The reward for good work is more work. When you show your appreciation and reward people, you automatically get to enjoy life more. Try to stay in the light, keeping your mind full of optimism and openness to new opportunities – personality traits which are associated with both total self-confidence and with humility. Mahatma Gandhi expressed it in the following way: "My people have left. I must follow them because I am their leader".

Who Can I Turn to for Help?

Remember the *Golden Rule of Networking*: Give without expecting anything in return. This may sound very altruistic, but in politics, business, and many areas of life – the old adage "it is not what you know, but who you know" is a lesson best learnt early in life. Networking is all about building and sustaining mutually beneficial relationships. It pays to start building relationships long before you think you will need them. This web of indebtedness represents a cluster of inter-dependencies and if you are in constant supply you are in constant demand.

I have a fantastic trick for you!

How do you react when people ask you for help? Chances are that you try to help. How do you feel afterwards? Chances are that you feel content. Most of us are flattered – either explicitly or implicitly – when asked for help. It's a sort of recognition of our competencies: You know something that I don't know. Cool! So the trick is to precondition your mind and persuade yourself that you are actually helping a person feel good about him- or herself when you ask for their help. You're making their day! For some reason most of us are better at helping others than at asking for help. Personally I don't remember a single instance when I have been let down when I have asked for help. The signal value of asking for help is humility and strength: I am self-aware and strong enough to recognize that you are better at this than me. At some point in time in our cultural development asking for help became interpreted as a sign of weakness, as an attack on our honor and competencies. My personal opinion is that the new generations are a lot better off about this issue. As digital natives they are used to seeking help in their network: Nothing is easier than asking for help on Facebook. There are no existential self-limitations in posting an open question on the internet: You will receive answers. That matter-of-factness could be beneficially transposed into our daily interactions with others. So start practicing asking straight-forward questions in a direct and outspoken way. We need to scale and to leverage intelligent networks in order to fully benefit from our collective intelligence.

Rob Cross from the McIntire School of Commerce, University of Virginia researches in the mapping of networks.[91] He has documented the importance of relationships for the information flow in organizations. Instead of accepting the usual hierarchical organizational diagrams at face value, he maps the actual information-based behavior. This network analysis leads to an identification of key people in the organization who are information centers. These influential people have a crucial impact on the results of the organization and, at the same time, represent a potential threat because the information networks collapse if they leave the organization. A shared characteristic of these information centers or knowledge owners is that they work across the silos. The role as knowledge owner has a lot in common with the integrator role. Neither of the roles appears explicitly on any job description, neither carries any formal authority but both roles have significant value for the organization.

Careers are built on both results and relationships. In your day-to-day work you are supported by many invisible hands that help you and support you without you necessarily realizing it. They are called colleagues! When you change your job you also change your network – in fact, for a while you will be without a support network. It is only when you can no longer take help for granted that you fully understand its value. Many executives only experience this sudden realization when they have changed jobs. When you change position, you abruptly realize that many issues in your former organization were solved without you being involved, because colleagues knew your preferences and decision styles, and loyally acted according to those. So, be aware of this when you move to a new job or a new organization.

In order to profile and position yourself you must be visible. You need to be out where the action is – that is best done in person and through social media. You need to contribute and share your views with others. That is what makes them grow. So one personal ambition for you might be to consume less of other people's lives on social media and produce more of your own life on social media. You may also learn a thing or two in the process. Therefore it is a good idea to join diverse societies and deliberately put yourself into a new challenging sensing position. If you don't have a point of view, get one! Try to consistently surprise others and not least yourself. Break into print and be visible online. Network actively and keep networking. You will be amazed by the amount of positive response and feedback that you will receive. That ongoing feedback will help you navigate and make quick course corrections.

> *"* The only thing worse than being talked about
> is not being talked about *"*
> *Oscar Wilde*

We all know the old proverb, *It is better to give than to receive* but perhaps this is only a part of the whole story. The beauty of helping is that the more you give, the more you get. So get used to helping people; develop your service gene – your caring gene. Be grateful – express gratitude and say thank you.

What is My Life Ambition?

I would like to introduce my *Personal Principles*: Purpose, Presence, and Flexibility. I want to be able to see the purpose of what I am doing. I want to be present in the execution of my activities. And I want to be flexible enough to be able to deviate from my planning when it becomes necessary. And then I want to have fun! My continuous challenge to myself is constantly being able to observe what is going on at the same time as carrying out the tasks – keeping a third-eye perspective. I am conscious that I will only be able to help people solve their issues by staying at a meta-level.

My journey towards this book began in 1996, when I was fired. After having spent 15 years specializing in marketing with global market leaders such as L'Oréal and The Coca-Cola Company, my life changed and I needed to reinvent myself. I had a wife and four children and my provider gene was challenged. Therefore, I wrote my first version of *The Personal Business Plan*. I still have it and it is still a guideline in my life. My creed at the time was Freedom, Independence, and Autonomy. So I chose to become a headhunter. Why? Because it would enable me to lead an inspiring work life and take my own destiny into my hands. As a headhunter you become better and better at what you do. And it is possible to gradually decrease work intensity over the years while performing at higher and higher levels.

Then, in 1999 I wrote a paper about "The Competition Concept of the Future – An Epochal Theory". The pragmatic reason for writing this paper was that it was needed to pursue my academic career – it was a requirement in order to become an External Lecturer at Copenhagen Business School. At the same time my desire was to create order in chaos. I wanted to conceive a stylish, holistic, qualitative, esthetic, and simple existential paradigm. For a long time I had been fascinated by meta-theories – even though I was well aware that it might seem futile to create an all-encompassing overview of this hypercomplex world. Chaos should not be looked at as an obstacle – rather as an opportunity. I was intrigued by the changes taking place and the emerging need for fundamental shifts in leadership style. By challenging ourselves, we grow stronger and more relevant to the people we serve. This led to the both/and concept.

I continued the journey by joining a one-year Meaningful Leadership PhD project in 2003. The project gave, and still gives me, valuable insight into what triggers success and happiness. The Danes are, according to numerous surveys, the happiest people in the world. When I started studying happiness in this context, I didn't know where it would lead me. It has been an extraordinary journey and I feel that my focus has led me to an extremely rewarding situation. I am happy. I live a fulfilling personal life and my professional life is highly stimulating. I practice four professional roles: Headhunter, Coach, Lecturer, and Author – with leadership as the pivotal center – and the Four-Leaf Clover has now become my guiding principle, my icon.

Inspiration: My Four Professional Roles

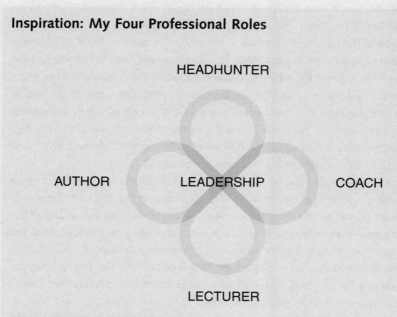

HEADHUNTER

AUTHOR   LEADERSHIP   COACH

LECTURER

Figure 17 My Four Professional Roles

The Four-Leaf Clover illustrates how my four professional roles support each other instead of competing with each other. I see myself with one foot placed at the center of the clover, pivoting around Leadership while I act in my four different professional roles. I see life as a continuous three-dimensional positive learning spiral with the four leaves as the foundation. It is only exciting for me as long as I continuously learn something new. I interact with some of the most interesting individuals on this planet, some of whom I recruit, some of whom I coach, some of whom I teach, and some of whom I write about. All in all, it's a highly inspirational and cross-fertilizing environment – our common challenge is to live life to the full and get the best out of it.

How would your own Four-Leaf Clover look around the central theme of reinvention? Use the template in the Appendix or at thepersonalbusinessplan. com. You will then discover elements of convergence in your life and see new connections between events you have until now seen as independent from each other. This will give you a new sense of purpose and guide your actions – specifically it will help you use the word "No" more effectively. It is always easy to accept new challenges and say "Yes" to new tasks – it is also socially desirable – however, for most people it is extremely hard to let go of old expertise and routine tasks. In the future your acid test will be: "On which leaf does this task belong and does it promote my vision of my future self?" If it doesn't, then your answer should be "No".

Think of the Four-Leaf Clover as a tool you use in order to relate the different roles you fill in your life to each other. First and foremost, look for synergies: How does one leaf support the others? Do you build leadership competencies by being chairman in your tennis club? Do you become a better communicator by writing letters to the editor? Can your interest in new technology give you an advance on the job market of the future? Can the fact that you are digitally savvy help your organization? And can your task of introducing and "on-boarding" new colleagues be developed into a teaching competency?

The ultimate goal must be to design a Four-Leaf Clover which supports your reinvention – which secures that you are moving and not stuck in *status quo*. You must frame some existential concepts which make you thrive and which support you in your long-term development. And please remember, that you never get tired when you work for yourself. Even when the exercise is successful you will still need to change the leaves from time to time. Personally, I worked in marketing for 15 years. Then, when I had emptied that development track I found a new one with its point of departure in my new situation. The Four-Leaf Clover is a tale that you tell yourself and which helps you see the meaning in the activities that you are carrying out. And in that process you become robust and 100 times more convincing. It is as if you have finally found yourself.

As mentioned, in 1996 I named my Personal Principles as Purpose, Presence, and Flexibility. While writing this book I somehow felt very much at ease with these principles, as if I had succeeded in living up to them. I therefore felt an urgent need to define an even more challenging life ambition:

I want to live happily until I become 100 years old.

Let me break my life ambition into parts.

I want to become 100 years old. No behavior can guarantee me a long life – of course I can become the victim of a deadly disease tomorrow. But I know what enhances my chances: I need to be in physical balance and mental balance. Both have consequences. First of all, I need to train my body by eating healthily and living an active life. Secondly, I need to take care of my psyche which means feeling comfortable financially and not letting my work life stress me significantly over longer periods of time. In order to remain highly efficient I have made a few choices: I run and swim every morning, I don't drink alcohol, I rarely spend time in front of the TV, and I don't focus on weather forecasts.

I want to be happy all the way. The word "happy" is really determining for my goal to be a candidate for a life ambition. Scientists more and more see a relation between inner happiness and physical health. But let me once and for all state that I am not content by reaching 100 years of age, if the years have passed by being on a diet and sweating at the gym. I have nothing against working hard, but I will not work so hard as to get a divorce. If I am to live happily then I know that I need good relationships, including a happy family life. On top of that I need a job that I find exciting, that makes me happy on a daily basis and that gives me a feeling of living my full potential.

I want to be able to reinvent myself. That I can only achieve by performing quantum leaps and achieving breakthroughs. I will not be forced to staying in a job if I am not happy in the morning when going to work. This part of my ambition has several consequences. It is an advantage to be financially independent but on top of that my competencies need to be mobile. What I am becoming good at should be usable in many contexts and in many ways. I have decided that I want to work to my death day – if I want to – even when becoming 100 years old. That goal necessitates that I follow new technologies and behaviors.

I can hardly express all the things that my life ambition has done for me. What it does in my daily life when making decisions. From the tiniest (I am tempted by a pastry, should I eat it or not?), over the bigger (should I keep teaching students in Corporate Communication even though the teaching each autumn lands in my calendar as a hand grenade?) to the biggest (should we move out of the country, when our kids move out of the house?).

Your life ambition should be as short as possible, one or two sentences. Then you may always write several pages about the consequences. For some of my clients the life ambition is ultra-short, for others a little longer. Sometimes I recommend a model where you simply state from where and where to you want to move. For example:

From corporate life to interesting discussion partner.

Your Life Quality

Does such a life ambition have consequences? Yes, definitely. It forces you to prioritize lifelong learning, even though it may seem hard at times. It motivates you to think about relationships and not only results. It also makes you explicitly put into words the value of simulating and feeding your curiosity each and every day, even though there always are reports to be read and meetings to be had. The crucial point is to keep a future perspective in all your actions. The point is not that the formulation of your life ambition should have some sort of special poetic quality. It should work as a practical tool for you. Don't fall in the trap where you think that your life ambition should be original. Freedom, love, control, and having fun are the key words for what is important in life.

Ambition is a combination of energy, will, and goals. In principle, it is about achieving a balance while meeting ambitious expectations through a combination of a disciplined approach to life and a rich emotional life. The most important thing is to work with your life quality and with what you have chosen to do. Identify the right things to be ambitious about and use your stamina to achieve your long term goal. You can determine whether your work activities constructively play together with your ambitions by asking: "What's in it for me?"

I am not a proponent of egotism. I sincerely believe that by solving your own issues, reducing your inner friction and becoming successful you will be able to make a difference in the life of others. And what is more important than making a difference to people who make a difference to you? By leveraging your own resources efficiently you become a role model and act as a catalyzing agent. Without vision there are no breakthroughs. Start by leading yourself, then the group and then the organization. Mahatma Gandhi said: "Be the change that you want to see in the world".

Inspiration: My Morning Ritual

Every morning at 6 am I rise and go for a run through the forest towards the beach. I dive into the sea while the sun rises. When I sit in the train on my way to work an hour later, I hugely enjoy it. To the left I look over the sea and to the right I have a deer park. Having arrived in the city I walk through a park with a fortress. I see a heron navigating through the trees and when it approaches it looks like a Boeing landing. Then I walk along the harbor before reaching my office near the Royal Castle.

This experience sits in my body the rest of the day. The fact that I have already had a string of beautiful experiences before even getting to work makes it difficult for others to knock me out. Some mornings I have interesting conversations on the train and some mornings I listen to music while walking. Music makes me happy. The forest, the sea, the sun, the deer, and the birds. The green, the blue, and the yellow. The heat in the body from jogging and the cold in the body from bathing. It is a ritual and it gives me energy. That is the way it is because that is the way I have decided it to be.

Because, of course, I also run through the rain on an ice-cold November morning. For one quarter of the year the deer park is dark as an abyss when I view it through the graffiti on the train window. Of course snow and storms make the walk along the harbor less poetic.

My morning ritual is a very simple example of the strength in a positive approach to every day.

The story fills me with energy. I look forward to the start of the new day when I lie down in bed, and I start my work day with significant energy and a smile on my lips.

In the labyrinth of today's leadership it is necessary to act as a heat-seeking missile and go directly after the target. It takes great leadership ability to penetrate the cultural codification and to cut through old habits. Immersion and reflection is the precondition for insight and self-awareness. In these individualistic times everybody has an opinion about everything. Distraction is overwhelming. It is only when you give yourself peace and quiet that you can see contexts and connections, and get an overview. You can't connect the dots when you're stressed. It is often under relaxed circumstances that the inspiration or solution comes – as though by itself. What would life look like if you reflected a bit more? Your brain simply operates in a different capacity when relaxed. It goes from beta-waves to alpha-waves with a lower frequency.[92] This corresponds to instant stress relief. When do you get your best ideas? Is it at the beginning of your holidays or towards the end? Please keep in mind that the best solution to a complex problem often is the simplest. Therefore, when the clutter is reduced, the solution often springs to mind. Seek greatness in simplicity.

Grow your key competencies and your distinctiveness – immerse yourself in the things you're best at. Reconciling opposing views and fostering creative solutions requires inclusiveness. And you need a fundamental knowledge of your strengths and weaknesses before you can map your opportunities and threats. By understanding your personal characteristics it becomes possible for you to use them in different ways in different situations and to fully exploit your situational leadership skills.

The power of the mind is overwhelming – make your subconscious mind work for you by priming it positively. Every time you say "but", it negates everything preceding it – so if you say "but" to a person, you can expect that nothing before the "but" will be understood or remembered.

Inspiration: Value Creation

Crown Prince Frederik of Denmark received some sound advice from his mother, Queen Margrethe II, "Be positive – look satisfied, when you move". That means hold your head high, walk affirmatively and show robustness. Everybody loves a cool, calm, and collected person. You assertively exercise your free will and you accept the consequences. Learn to present your life ambition as a function of the value it creates for others. How would you answer if you were asked "In what ways will the realization of your life ambition benefit me?"? Grandiose examples of possible answers are Jeff Bezos' Amazon creed "Everything, Everybody, Everywhere" and Bill Gates' Microsoft mantra "Everything that can think will link".

In this era of globalization where we compete with more people from more countries in more ways than ever before, maybe it is the question "Why?" that can give us the individual and collective energy we need to compete effectively. We must have a common goal and a shared understanding of our activities. It is the responsibility of the top executive to formulate and communicate both the direction and the ambition level of the organization. In this, hypercomplexity is your enemy; you need to develop and practice the ability to see around corners, reduce uncertainty and create clarity.

A good example of the magnitude of the challenge is L'Oréal which has achieved a record 20 years of consecutive double digit profit growth. Lindsay Owen-Jones, L'Oréal's CEO during the whole period has perfected L'Oréal's strategy and business model which is to buy local beauty brands, give them a makeover, and distribute them globally.[93] Another special feature of the L'Oréal business approach is to introduce new innovative formulas through the top exclusive brands like Lancôme and then allow them to trickle down in a cascade effect through the other divisions of the organization. This ensures a multitude of product launches that keep up dynamism – not forgetting internal competition. As soon as a division of the organization reaches a certain size it is split up in order to make it compete within the parent company. It makes the organization feel small, even if it isn't. I can't help signaling the bitter irony in the choice of the word division. Sounds a bit ominous, don't you think?

Jeffrey Immelt, the CEO of GE, provides another illustration of the sheer size of the challenge facing present day top executives. In order to achieve the stated growth objectives and fulfill market expectations, GE needs to annually add business to the tune of the revenue of Nike! This unquestionably demands a clear vision, a focused mindset and a creative attitude. But how can it be done? Let's have a look at some of the factors in play.

The child's quest for the parents' recognition and praise is transformed, in adult life, to the ambition to do well, become rich and be respected. Many male corporate leaders are marked by the lack of a loving relationship with their father. So now, 40 years later, they sit as apparently successful people and repeat "Dad, look at me!" while they fight in vain for the love of their father, who may be long dead.

In coaching sessions with top leaders, I try to establish a gentle and responsive dialogue. I see coaching as taking a valued person from where they are to where they want to be. I have gotten used to the fact that what I am presented with at first is not the real reason. Sometimes it helps using a tool borrowed from project management called *Five Times Why?* It is a question-asking technique used to explore the cause-and-effect relationships underlying a particular problem. The primary goal of the technique is to determine the root cause of a problem.

Inspiration: Five Times Why

If you have difficulties in defining what you are struggling with, take your immediate answers to the first three questions of your Personal Business Plan (What baggage from the past must I let go of? What is meaningful to me right now? and How can I move forward?). Then ask yourself the most simple and effective follow-up question of our language:

"Why?"

Write down your answer.

Repeat the exercise five times.

You will no doubt get to the core of something important. Most of the people I meet first answer with a formulation that is well-known to them, which they are used to using when discussing with friends or colleagues. If you are frustrated by too much traveling, then *Five Times Why?* will show you the road to a much more significant recognition.

"I am tired of having so many days of travel in my job."

Why?

"It is strenuous to travel."

Why?

"There is all the preparation, packing and ironing, and there is the time differences that are killing me."

Why is that a problem?

"I don't ever get to be home, before I have to leave again. I feel that I am simply in a transfer."

Why is that a problem?

"Mostly I'm tired when I am with my wife and I hardly get to see my friends. Many of them I haven't seen in half a year."

Why is that a problem?

"I'm lonely."

There are significant differences in fundamental attitude depending on your position in the family. Firstborn children in the family very often develop a strong drive to hunt. After the arrival of a sibling, the child perceives that it must fight in order to earn and retain the recognition of the parents. They often grow into leaders who give orders, are competitive, and have a natural authority. The younger siblings will often, working in a team, think outside the box, be imaginative, and willing to follow orders. They tend to focus more on relationships and social capital.

Both leadership styles are needed. If you want to have success in business and in life you need to create a stimulating environment and energizing relationships; these will give you both cross-fertilization and inspiration. You must focus on the long run; life is a marathon, not a sprint. In my reinvention perspective I look at life as a relay – you continually deliver the baton to the next version of yourself – following the road leading to serial mastery. Think of the challenges, the relationships and your results as pit stops that replenish your energy reserves and break your day-to-day routine. Madonna expresses it in the following way: "No matter who you are, no matter what you did, no matter where you've come from, you can always change, become a better version of yourself".

A central challenge for all leaders is to establish stretch targets that motivate and create energy. Bill Bowerman, the legendary runner and coach who started the running wave in USA with his book *Jogging* from 1967, was once asked by Phil Knight, founder of Nike: "How do I run faster?" The answer was: "Triple your speed".[94] This is another good example of an exemplary partnership. Phil Knight took care of the business end of Nike whereas Bill Bowerman as co-founder took care of product development and innovation. In Microsoft it is Steve Balmer who runs the business and Bill Gates who was the Chief Strategist. As in life, a trusted partner is crucial for success in business. Identify and find your partner – it is the best investment of time you can make.

The courage to commit yourself – on behalf of yourself and your organization – is also crucial to success. You must dare to make decisions and accept that you will never be in a position to obtain full knowledge. By working consistently towards an ambitious goal, the top executive ensures that the choices made become the right ones. It has been described as the ability to see around corners but you may also visualize life as a decision tree with numerous branches. At any specific time you must make a choice and delete some alternative options. History seldom shows that the alternative could have been a better choice. This is perhaps what made Winston Churchill say "History will be kind to me for I intend to write it". Further, when asked what he considered the most essential qualification for a politician, Churchill replied "It is the ability to foretell what will happen tomorrow, next month and next year – and to explain afterward why it did not happen".

Flemming's Tale: His New Life

Flemming's Life Ambition had now become:

> **To be a stimulating dialogue partner to develop the creative interaction between government, civic society and the corporate sector – the catalytic society.**
>
> **To have a particular emphasis on people, cities and buildings.**

In order to live out his ambition he had carefully planned ahead and had taken upon him several global positions of trust enabling him to build his future Catalytic Society platform:

- Chairman of the Danish Architecture Center (DAC)
- President of International Federation of Housing and Planning (IFHP)
- Governing Council Member of European Foundation Center (EFC)
- Urban Design Committee Chair of Mission Design Montreal
- Ambassador of UN Global Compact
- Council Member of World City Prize Singapore

Flemming also put up several other ambitious challenges for himself. In this Decade of Morality he wanted to live with total integrity and alignment between his words and his actions. He would contribute with his special blend of financial expertise, knowledge of the voluntary sector and philanthropic insight. He would as long as possible continue working on the boards of Realdania related organizations. He defined himself as a founding father of the Catalytic Society. He chose to build a company together with his wife. He would use his successful existential platform for giving back. He also chose to let go a little – evolve from Mister Perfect to Mission Perfect – perform with relaxed readiness. Consciously he also accepted risk – everything else would be un-ambitious and boring. In short he was morphing into a new and improved version of himself: Flemming 7.0.

Jan's Tale: His Short-Term Plan

First of all Jan wanted to build a plan for his CSC future with his direct superior, a trusted boss who was very appreciative of Jan's professionalism. The path forward through an expat career with CSC needed to be evaluated. Then the path forward through the mentor program, a High Potential program and the possibility of an MBA needed to be scrutinized. One of his challenges and focus areas was delegation, delegation and delegation. He needed to ensure both doing things right and doing the right things. He clearly experienced that each time he himself became a producer, things tended to slow down and the quality became lower. He had become a bottleneck. He also had to trust that others would eventually take up orphan tasks – nature abhors a vacuum – so if he became unavailable, then others would take over. Finally he needed to focus more on managing up – he needed to flag his performance – which was counter-intuitive due to his natural humility.

Key Learning

- Don't declare, deliver.
- Remain learning agile – seek new experiences.
- Take the road less traveled – differentiate yourself.
- Demonstrate your strengths by using the STAR model: Situation, Task, Action, and Result.
- Develop the right competencies – they will follow you for the rest of your life.
- Think of your actions as using opportunities rather than making sacrifices – you're not a victim.
- At work you deal with tasks surrounded by feelings; in the private sphere you deal with feelings surrounded by tasks.
- Define your Personal Principles and your Life Ambition.
- Focus, Focus, Focus.
- Build up the necessary courage to fully committing yourself.

8

How Do I Differentiate Myself from Others?

> *"When you reach for the stars you might not quite get one,
> But you will not come up with a handful of mud, either"*
> *Leo Burnett*

I cannot overemphasize the importance of realizing that nobody will manage your career for you. You must take absolute responsibility for yourself. The trick is to apply your professional techniques and toolbox to your personal life. Sometimes this means disengaging. It also means seeking continuous feedback; communication is collaborative and the more you listen to others the more you learn about yourself. However, the borderline between internal and external communication is becoming more and more blurred. This distinction seems less and less relevant – new communication technologies promote transparency and the inner picture needs to correspond to the outer. This produces a holistic perspective. You probably evaluate personal and professional feedback using the same criteria as you apply when you evaluate news: Importance, topicality, relevance, conflict and sensation. Some feedback is deemed to be more relevant and so it touches you more. Be aware of these repeated themes and do your utmost to articulate exactly why they touch you. When you have found these reasons you might have identified some of the reasons behind the "mysteries" in relation to your former interactions.

Forced Writing Exercise: My Personal Feedback

Take 6½ minutes to write down personal feedback that has really meant something to you. Don't stop writing. For inspiration you may use the stakeholders mentioned in the Happiness 360 degree model: Partner, children, parents, relatives, friends, community, boss, peers, and employees. Think back and focus on all the comments that you have received over time. Single out the salient messages and try to identify the overall themes. Remember that you already know the themes perfectly well, it's just a question of getting them down on paper. Looking at these themes is it possible for you to identify any hints at your blind spots?

Don't be afraid of committing yourself. Your ability to commit is a crucial element of your success – both in your professional and in your personal life. In the latter, finding a partner and sticking with him/her creates a stable core around which your life can evolve. Even though you wish to commit to activities, projects, and ambitions outside your personal relationship, you must make room for each other and ensure that you have the emotional and mental energy to sustain this vital partnership. You need both to generate and to regenerate.

In recent years, I have sensed a tendency among men to use their emotional vocabulary more than they used to do; conversely women are using their rational vocabulary more and more. This evolution could certainly reduce many of the misunderstandings and tensions in life. On a trip to Greenland, I once met a representative from an Arctic women's network. She drew my attention to a piece of advice for women who want to have a career: "Speak like a man!" It surprised me at first but upon closer reflection I understood that it was about basing one's communication on rationality and results, and focusing on product rather than process. Reservations tend to weaken the impact of a message. Top executives need to reduce uncertainty by communicating with unreserved clarity. However, the holistic softer female approach is increasingly gaining traction, giving room for more nuances and reservations, maybe leading to more viable and thought-through decisions?

The concept of the glass ceiling stems from an article in *Adweek* in 1984 and is hence almost 30 years old. Considering the economic, technological, and ideological development that has since taken place it is not surprising that the metaphor seems outdated. Instead, perhaps we should talk about a glass elevator. As in all elevators, there is space for a maximum number of passengers who want to go to the top. In order to get in and out of the elevator it is necessary to be at the right place when it stops. In business this demands an active effort to make your competencies visible – you must want to *and* be able to ride the wave.

In order to secure the future of the organization it is absolutely necessary to recruit female leaders. To disregard half the population would, in these Talent Management and Risk Management times, look like a real handicap. Looking at it from a purely commercial viewpoint, it is also interesting to gain insight into female decision-making processes and buying behavior since a greater and greater share of household consumption is managed by women. Women in the executive team often contribute to an improvement of teamwork and communication and, finally, women tend to prioritize the care dimension higher than their male counterparts. Even though there is still a long way to go, we have come a long way. In 2013 the CEOs of the following internationally known companies were women: Avon Products, DuPont, Harpo, HP, Kraft Foods, PepsiCo, Sara Lee, Xerox, and Yahoo.

In the final analysis, organizations choose the most competent leader for the top executive position. Work life is a meritocracy where it is the results that determine the career. The fundamental challenge for female leaders therefore is to document results and to protect their own interests instead of merely performing by excellently solving the case. From an executive search consultant's perspective there is significant positive signal value related to an ambitious female leader building her character.

In the following box, I have listed a few suggestions of how you can improve your career. Depending on your specific lifecycle situation some will be more relevant than others. Feel free to pick and choose in order to improve your own career.

Inspiration: The A–Z for a Better Career

- Apply for a job in an organization of a certain size, a strong position and a global anchoring. Its focus should be on growth and development.
- Behave – be cultured.
- Create solid relationships – get along and get ahead.
- Dress well and appropriately – look the part. It is vital to create a positive impression from the first moment.
- Educate yourself and remember – your functional professionalism must be excellent before you start discussing general management.

Formulate your *raison d'être*.

Global perspective – become multicultural. Obtain an authentic global perspective through your education, your work experiences, and so on.

Have both style and substance.

Initiative – take initiatives, be result oriented, flexible and honest. Stand up for yourself – also in headwind and finish each job properly.

Job change – it is self-improvement.

Know thyself – be honest with yourself. Do not lie, least of all to yourself.

Listen to your intuition – it is the sum of your experiences.

Mentoring – choose a competent mentor – listen to her/him.

Navigate in networks – make full use of business alliances. Create networks and alliances. Establish a network – also outside your organization.

Optimism – history never shows the alternative. Express yourself in positives.

Perform – create visible results – focus on the target. Seek challenges and perform visible results.

Quality – remember that quality never goes out of style.

Results – remember to relate your effort to the result of the organization.

Seek challenges both internally and externally. It is permitted to try out things early in your career – later it is necessary to demonstrate solid results through the long haul. Grab the exciting challenges – be proactive.

Take care – your health and your family should also stand the distance.

Uniqueness – remember that the key to success is differentiation.

Value your independence and circle of influence.

Willingness to change – you are not afraid of changing but of being changed.

X is a symbol that marks the spot where you are. Be aware of the here and now.

"Yes" is more – engage in new disruptive challenges and you will become a better you.

Zen is an attitude – detach yourself from your emotions and you will become a better leader.

What am I Better at than Anybody Else?

Talent is overrated.[95] There seems to be a growing, common understanding between researchers regarding the role of talent which comes down to the realization that what really separates world-class performers from everybody else is deliberate practice and hard work. Planning and dedication is also a factor. Tiger Woods was the world's first sports dollar billionaire.[96] He started playing golf at the age of three and a half! Gary Player – a legend among golfers and business people alike – offered the well-known aphorism "The more you practice, the luckier you get". Henry Ford said: "It has been my understanding that most people get ahead during the time that others waste". To take an example from the animal kingdom: A shark never sleeps, if it did so it would sink to the ocean floor. It is created for motion during its entire lifespan.

Malcolm Gladwell in his book *Outliers – The Story of Success* convincingly illustrates this point by documenting that The Beatles between 1960 and 1964 played for 10 000 hours in small clubs in Hamburg.[97] They played eight hours a night, seven days a week and this was where that they learned to be The Beatles.[98] Bill Gates went to one of the few public schools with student access to a computer. When he decided to drop out of college he had already been programming for 10 000 hours.[99]

This focus on deliberate practice and mastery neatly fits with one of my favorite quotes from Margaret Mead: "A small group of thoughtful people could change the world. Indeed, it is the only thing that ever has". If you have a strength-in-depth sense of a cause that is worth fighting for then there are no limits to where you can go and what you can do. The only things that hold you back are your own self-limitations. If you really believe that you're right, then go for it! This would apply whether you are In Search Of Excellence, In Search Of Talent, or In Search Of Happiness.

Don't quit when the going gets tough. Persistence will always win the day, even over talent and intelligence – and you will demonstrate staying power. Talent helps, but it will not take you as far as ambition. Success in top management demands as much energy and maturity as it does knowledge and skills – and perseverance. Or, as Harley-Davidson puts it: "It's not the age; it's the mileage". Success comes partly through diligent execution of the basics. Furthermore, the structural demand for top talent increases more than the economic demand decreases so, even in times of crisis, there will be additional demands for leaders. This is based simply on structure and demography. And, as you probably know, demographics is the mother of all trends. We are now witnessing a silver tsunami.

The Cold War for Talent means that when you recruit in the future, you will have to look for three qualities in excellent candidates:

1. Integrity
2. Intelligence
3. Energy.

And, as Warren Buffett says if the first one is lacking, the second two will kill you. John W. Gardner adds: "In hiring key employees, look only for two qualities: Judgment and taste. There's plenty of nearly everything else".

The Cold War for Talent is risk management. To utilize all necessary means to attract the best people is a strategic decision which needs to be taken at the highest possible level in the organization. It's not only about achieving the best possible bottom line; it is about being able to obtain a positive bottom line at all. Top executives usually have high and clearly formulated ambitions for the organization. From a leadership point of view there is more and more focus on execution rather than on vision. This is probably because many great visions have drowned in failed execution.

> // A man of knowledge lives by acting,
> not by thinking about acting,
> nor by thinking about what he will think
> when he is finished acting //
> Carlos Castaneda[100]

People who say "It cannot be done" shouldn't interrupt people who are doing it. It is also the case that sustained business superiority stems not so much from decisions about strategy as from decisions about people. The greatest decisions are not about What? but about Who? You can't keep cream from rising to the top. People who are conventionally clever get jobs based on their qualifications (the past), not on their desire to succeed (the future). The power of the past comes from experience; the power of the future is born from experiment. Nike has a take on this. In an early advertisement for their trendy high-tech Shox shoe series, the text reads:

> You know, sometimes I ask myself, 'What happened to the future, they promised us?' We are well into the 21st century and still we have no jetpacks. Where are the undersea colonies, food powder and amphibious cars? Furthermore, why am I not living in a split-level home on Mars and watching the big game on a TV the size of my fingernail? Where are the three-minute milers, four-metre high jumpers, and 500-km marathons? And where are the robot swimmers complete with oxybreathability? Just think about it. Has the world lived up to these promises? In a word 'No'. Sure we have the Internet and stuff like that, but I want to know what happened to the pills that, right in front of your eyes, turn into pets when you add water and why my computer does not have a sexy personality like the ones from those futuristic movies? Now that would be a cool thing.[101]

Talent management has a built-in paradox. Talent is about development, energy, passion and potential. Management is about channeling this potential, but carries the inherent risk that the freshness and spontaneity disappears in the process. So the more you try to control an inherently creative process, the more you risk destroying it.

I would like to repeat that nobody will manage your career for you. Your career lies in your own hands. You are the one who has to make the choices. To give you some help with a qualitative approach to career planning, I include a list of questions from the AESC regarding self-improvement and talent philosophy:[102]

- What are you doing to improve your knowledge and skills?
- How will you acquire the experience necessary to achieve your long-term goal, for example to become a CEO?
- What experience, responsibilities and personal qualifications will make you a candidate – what "pieces" do you still need?
- What is the most important attribute (only one) in a potential candidate, when you hire a leader?

⊗ If there are two equally qualified candidates for a job, what determines your final choice?

⊗ What personality and style characterize the people, who get promoted and/or seem to be the most recognized in your organization?

⊗ If an employee was asked which adjective most precisely describes the personality of the best employees, what would he or she say?

⊗ If a client was asked to describe the culture in your organization, what would he or she say?

⊗ How do you handle employees who do not perform?

⊗ Who is seen to be the most valuable employee in your organization? Which typical characteristics and traits does he or she have?

⊗ How are bigger decisions taken? Is it by consensus, by majority or by an individual?

⊗ What do you expect a good employee to have as a general ambition in the career?

⊗ What must an employee do or show in order to be considered for promotion?

Some of the themes are illustrated in the Egg Model.

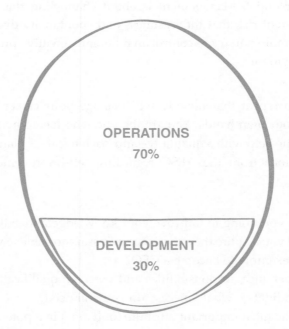

Figure 18 The Egg

The Egg Model was developed by Paul Evans, Shell Chaired Professor of Human Resources and Organizational Development at INSEAD and describes your typical tasks as a leader: 70% is Operations (Execution) and 30% Development.[103] You are hired to fulfill the demands and carry out the tasks at hand – doing that is what you get your salary for. You get promoted by taking initiatives, starting projects, stretching your role and responsibility, focusing on the interest of the organization, ensuring alignment between you, your boss and your boss's boss, and seeing your own position in the big picture.

Your success is closely related to your willingness to assume responsibility. I once had the opportunity to recruit a COO for an industrial corporation. During the conversations it became obvious that the CEO had an issue with a new product area and that he had promised to deliver a strategic plan to the Board. This had not yet happened. It was discussed during the interviews but nothing was put in writing. The new COO started and three months later, I asked him how things were going. His answer was that everything was okay and relationships were positive all the way around. I then asked him if he was working on the strategic plan for the new product area and he told me that he had not had the time. I then had to tell him that as the CEO was already late with the strategic plan at the time of the recruitment, then the COO was now very late and I went as far as saying that this might constitute a serious limiting factor regarding his career. Realizing this, the COO asked me how he could prioritize this urgent and important task. We then went through an exercise called *calendar hygiene*. I sat down with him and we went through all his appointments and discussed where his presence was necessary, which meetings he could delegate and which he could simply cancel. By prioritizing according to financial goals, new-product goals, and people goals, this simple exercise gave him enough space to finish the strategic plan within one month. It never became the career limiting factor that was in the cards, had he not responded adequately.

What Else Differentiates Me from the Rest?

The question in the last section was "What am I better at than anybody else?" The word "different" rather than "better" adds another qualitative level to the understanding of the question and the message it conveys. The value you contribute in a specific context is leveraged by the degree to which you are different. There is value in diversity. Tom Peters takes it even further: "Be distinct or extinct". The renowned former president and CEO of The Coca-Cola Company, Roberto C. Goizueta famously said "The three keys to selling consumer products are differentiation, differentiation and differentiation". Bill Gates has recounted that he dropped out of college reluctantly: "Unlike some students, I loved college. However, I felt the window of opportunity to start a software company might not open again". He felt compelled to embark on the right highway immediately.

We all suffer from the threat of being commoditized – there are no guarantees when (and not if) the rules change. Minimalism and opt out is a current trend. Many individuals choose to opt out of the "work, buy, consume, die" lifestyle. This is one way of differentiating yourself and breaking through the self-limitations and dependencies that you might have created over time.

When observing our changing environment the paradigm thinking of Thomas Kuhn[104] (in an updated form) becomes relevant and useful:

- ⊗ Paradigms filter reality.
- ⊗ Paradigms are usual.
- ⊗ Paradigms are useful.
- ⊗ Paradigms are warnings.
- ⊗ New paradigms are created by outsiders – they have nothing to lose.
- ⊗ Paradigm pioneers must be brave – trust in faith.
- ⊗ Beware of paradigm paralysis – be yourself.
- ⊗ Culture gaps are perceptions of differences between paradigms.

Forced Writing Exercise: The Paradigm Question

Take 6½ minutes and, using forced writing, answer the paradigm question: What looks impossible today, but if it could be done, would fundamentally change your position to the better? This involves going back to zero and start all over again – there is always another solution to a given problem. Do not stop writing, associations will come.

It was Alan Kay, a young computer scientist at Xerox, who said: "The best way to predict the future is to invent it". The Alto computer was the brainchild of Alan Kay and his researchers who foresaw early on that computers would become more than digital calculators. He was interested in proving his ideas by working on interactive educational systems for children. He had been playing with and talking about the idea of a portable machine he called a Dynabook (anticipating many features of the laptop). Yet in 1972 his idea for building a computer to teach children was rejected by a Xerox lab manager who dismissed the idea as being too far outside the research center's charter.

Robert Kegan goes all the way by stating that "We shall not solve the problems, we shall let the problems solve us". It's important to work through the problem, not just skirt around them. We need to focus on the future even though it may seem overwhelming. Your authentic individual focus will create aspirational breakthroughs.

How Good Do I Want to Be?

A former Managing Director of McKinsey&Company once said that McKinsey people are "insecure overachievers". In context it was clear that he regarded being an insecure overachiever as something to be proud of. To this day, a number of McKinsey people let that description define their mindset and behaviors. McKinsey&Company deliberately recruit consultants who can be categorized in this way. It describes young, moldable, and brilliant people who have relatively little self-confidence and therefore need to prove themselves over and over again. You can't find a much more powerful motivator than this – and everybody wins!

I would suggest that to offer meaningful work is the greatest motivator in the world. And in this context it may be fruitful to use Quadrant II[105] thinking (please refer to figure 19). This involves categorizing tasks and decisions according to their urgency and their importance.

The tasks and decisions in the first quadrant are both urgent and important. You are seldom in doubt about these. They could include specific assignments from your largest customer, your boss or the board.

Secondly, there are the urgent, but not important tasks and decisions. They often take up precious time simply because of their urgency. They are important to the people at the other end but not to you – meaning they do not contribute to your success criteria. However, since you are polite and helpful, you usually

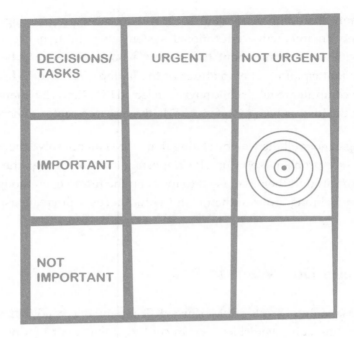

Figure 19 Quadrant II

find time for these activities. There is also a certain satisfaction in simply getting things done.

Then we have the not urgent and not important tasks and activities. Even though we all want to appear highly efficient, we all waste time occasionally. We drink a cup of coffee; we chat with others, read the newspaper, surf the web, or simply daydream. However, these activities may also serve regenerative or social purposes, so we should not just disregard them.

Finally we have the last quadrant, Quadrant II, where the not urgent, but important tasks and decisions are found. This is where value is created. If you go back to the Egg in the first section of this chapter, you will remember that the 30% dedicated to development and initiatives was what got you promoted. This means performing activities that were not included in your job description or, in short, over-delivering. In Quadrant II nobody asks you to deliver. The tasks and decisions can always be delayed because there is no deadline – and in practice this is usually what happens. The important but not urgent tasks and decisions get postponed. From an organizational perspective this means that the strategic plan for a new, small but highly promising market is not made or that the extra "relationship building" call to a potential customer is not made. Nobody will criticize you for delaying these activities – actually because nobody else knows that you should be doing them.

From a personal perspective though, the consequences may be more severe. Among the not urgent but important tasks and decisions on your personal agenda are:

⊗ To take care of each of your family members, when especially needed.
⊗ To continually learn – for example, to participate in executive education.
⊗ To choose and cherish your life partner.
⊗ To develop your core competencies.
⊗ To make your dream come true.
⊗ To identify your blind spots.
⊗ To build a fulfilling career.
⊗ To get rid of your fear.
⊗ To be in control.
⊗ To be happy.

In order to make the model operational for you personally, allocate your total work time to these four quadrants. Be honest with yourself. Take a few minutes to think it through and write a percentage in each of the quadrants. With today's work and organizational pressure, I would not be surprised if you ended up with 60% in urgent and important, 25% in urgent and not important, 10% in not-urgent and not important (don't kid yourself – you also need to survive) and only 5% in Quadrant II, not urgent and important. Considering that it is in this Quadrant II that your personal value is generated this finding might seem a little frustrating. But there are ways out. One is to perform the calendar hygiene that I already described. Another is to think holistically about the Quadrant II concept. People around you also have their Quadrant II; luckily, some of the activities that are urgent and not important to you might be urgent and important to them. You may be able to delegate some of these tasks and decisions and, in doing so, create meaningful work for your colleagues. Your aim should be to dedicate at least 20% of your time to Quadrant II. This will inevitably lead to a change in your behavior. You will become more of a mentor, you will become more reflective and you will create more value for yourself and your organization. All disruptive initiatives originate in Quadrant II. All business breakthroughs originate in Quadrant II. All human breakthroughs originate in Quadrant II. By taking up the Quadrant II challenge you will really feel that you are in the driver's seat.

One of the key questions you need to ask yourself is: "What is in it for me?" When you analyze new tasks or decisions always take into account whether they contribute to your success criteria: If not then they should be delegated. Another key determinant is the quantitative versus the qualitative time dimension. The ancient Greeks had two words for time – *chronos* and *kairos*. While the former refers to chronological or sequential time, the latter signifies a time "in between", an undetermined moment of time in which something special happens. What that special something is depends entirely on who is using the word. While *chronos* is quantitative, *kairos* is qualitative in nature. It means the right or opportune moment (the supreme moment). This concept might actually be what Claus Otto Scharmer was thinking of when he expounded his Theory U. Quadrant II is most certainly *kairos* time. If you have children, you have already realized that there is no quality time, only real time. You cannot just switch on an authentic relationship to your child; it takes time and availability, allowing the child to choose when he/she wants to enter into a dialogue. Similarly, in order to perform in Quadrant II you need to maintain a receptive and balanced mode that allows you to sense when it's the right moment to make your move. Quadrant II is about prioritizing both your time and your actions so you achieve the optimal result. It is important to have a bias towards action. My personal preference is to front-load tasks and maintain a sense of urgency. I want to keep up speed and momentum. I always feel that time is of essence and therefore I anchor my daily activities in my calendar according to Quadrant II.

In the greater scheme of things Quadrant II is also about how you want to be remembered. What sort of things, both tangible and intangible, do you want to leave behind? Stephen R. Covey puts it in the following way: "Life is short, so love, live, learn and leave a legacy".[106] You have never seen a tombstone with the following inscription: "I wish I had spent more time at the office!" The archetypical entrepreneur would probably write: "I am working on a comeback!"

Leadership presence is described as a package of intangibles such as passion, social poise, energy, communication skills and appearance – and these are what ultimately lead you to a senior executive appointment. Remember that no matter how good your financial and business credentials, and how impressive your achievements, these are only the minimum requirements – the price of admission competencies. It is your intangible qualities that will drive your success as a leader. What is really critical in becoming a successful leader is integrity and boardroom appearance; the ability to present the right ideas effectively and the capacity to take ownership in making things happen. This demand for the less tangible personal attributes has driven the proliferation of psychometric assessment. My best estimate is that psychometric assessment adds 10–15% to the quality of an expert evaluation of a professional. It permits you to add a few dimensions and highlight a few more themes and thus, always creates value in the process. The finding will provide useful hypotheses and permit a closer look into the decision dynamics of the individual.

Flemming's Tale: "How Do I Stand Out?"

Flemming put forward some significant differentiators. First of all, he defined himself as inclusive and tolerant. He cared about others and welcomed new ideas and perspectives. He didn't play defense and used power when needed. He emphasized honor. He was organizationally savvy and liked working in complex business environments – it gave him energy. He was creative and would work on being even more spontaneous. He was an inspiring communicator and excelled at building bridges between people and audiences. Finally – he was not humble.

Jan's Tale: "What's in It for Me?"

Jan decided to emanate his role models. He also decided to have a more pragmatic view on his career. It was no longer enough solving the tasks and creating the solutions. It was also necessary that there should be some value in it for Jan. So he would try to live more after the "What's in it for me?" mantra even though it didn't seem totally natural to him. His generous and professional attitude would – if not moderated – have led him to simply doing what was necessary regardless of the benefit to him. The process of documenting his activities and results in his Personal Business Plan led him to this crucial discovery.

Key Learning

- Regarding your career you're on your own – people are dictated by self-interest.
- Work life is a meritocracy where it is the results that determine the career.
- Maintain a global perspective – become multicultural.
- Listen to your intuition – it is the sum of your experiences.
- Choose a competent mentor.
- Be aware of the here and now.
- Talent is overrated – what really separates world-class performers from everybody else is deliberate practice and hard work.
- Focus on development, not only operations – that will get you promoted.
- Focus on Quadrant II: The not urgent but important stuff – that will make you happy.
- Get rid of your fear.

9

What is My Personal Business Plan?

// The future, as always, belongs to the brave //
Bill Bernbach

Try to develop a mental picture of two identities: One is a trusted advisor and the other is a racing driver who barely succeeds in keeping the car on track in the turns. One exudes calmness and the other exudes hyperactivity. Accept ambiguity and accept that there are no clear-cut answers. You have to find your own answers by exploring your foundation. When you know yourself you have no enemies. Behind every frustration lies an ambition. It is not a breakdown, it is a breakthrough. It is like taking a conscious decision to pass through a threshold or a doorway. The basketball star Michael Jordan puts it in this way: "Limits, like fears, are often just an illusion".

Think of your Personal Business Plan as a business logic. It needs to function in a way that fulfills the demands for flexibility (short-term), adaptability (long-term) and concordance about your goals. This is exactly the framework for the corporation's sustained competitiveness known as Triple A: Agility, Adaptability, and Alignment:

- *Agility*: to be able to respond to short-term changes in order to handle external disruptions smoothly.
- *Adaptability*: to be able to adjust to structural shifts in the markets.
- *Alignment*: to create incentives for better performance.

In your case alignment is about reducing friction between your goals and the goals of your environment. It is possible for you to set up a goal that overpowers the limitations that are built into your environment. Your life ambition has made the limitations irrelevant, simply because the limitations are temporary whereas your life ambition is permanent. At any point in time you are able to define in what way your individual actions contribute to the realization of your life ambition. This creates a feeling of invulnerability. You are in the driver's seat and able to squeeze meaning out of your daily actions. It doesn't matter what the others think – you are moving confidently your own way – trusting that your business logic will trump the short term obstacles. It takes 10 years of hard work to become an overnight success!

Sometimes we are so busy with business that we could think of ourselves as human *doings* instead of human *beings*. You can't think clearly when you're stressed or panicking. All your creative potential is drowned by adrenaline and you act within the confines of your own self-limitations. One anecdote comes to mind. President Ronald Reagan, when confronted with crisis, either real or imagined, used a catchphrase when his advisors were all rushing around: "Don't just do something – stand still!" Calmness is an acquired behavior that you can achieve if you connect with your core and remain grounded. Reduce nervous energy by balancing your hectic lifestyle with deliberation. Reduce the tension in your inner spring and reduce the inner pressure. Reduce the speed of your body, that is, your metabolism – this will also make you live longer. We have no harsher judges than ourselves.

When you stop running after the agenda of other people you will experience a state of empowerment. You will feel that it is possible for you to create your own category instead of competing against others with unclear and changing success criteria. Your success criteria should be aligned with your core business, not only pleasing your bosses. Bosses and businesses change, your life ambition remains.

Inspiration: Finding Value in What You Do

Actor Stig Rossen[107] has had more than 700 performances as Jean Valjean in *Les Misérables* in theaters all over the world. His usual daytime rhythm was broken because he came home late and full of adrenaline after the last performance. He also noticed at one point that he was demotivated and felt as if he were navigating on autopilot due to performing the same show over and over again. He needed to take action and found new energy by realizing that it was never the same show. There were always differences. One evening, the bass player had two socks of different colors on. One evening the female star had a new hairstyle. One evening one of the singers had a cold. Focusing on diversity and small differences, instead of uniformity and repetition, helped him come through all the shows with a sense of meaning. Each detail was important for the construction of the whole, and the whole was never identical to the precedent construction. Stig Rossen worked seriously with himself on changing the circumstances by creating variations and improvements from within. Every day he made small adjustments to his makeup, acting, and singing. The lesson here is to find value in what you do and to identify your specific and unique contribution.

How Can I Reinvent Myself in Order to Remain Relevant?

Your vision of where or who you want to be is the greatest asset you have. If you were a brand, what would people say about you. In other words: What is your Personal Brand? Give yourself some spin. Don't give a speech. Put on a show. Improve your strike rate. How you perceive yourself is how others will see you. Be interesting, tell the truth, and live the truth.

The typical branding approach is first to define the market, then to quantify the segment, and lastly, to create the brand. Paradoxically, the function responsible for branding is just about the only function in the organization that has not rebranded itself over the years. After 60 years, Marketing is still called Marketing.

Peter Drucker,[108] who has been called the man who invented management, said that "The business enterprise has two – and only these two – basic functions: marketing and innovation. Marketing and innovation produce results; all the rest are costs". Marketing is scratching, before it itches, making subliminal needs explicit. Gary Hamel wrote in *Leading the Revolution*[109] that Silicon Valley is a natural place to seek inspiration. Silicon Valley is a meritocracy in which the best argument wins. It does not matter who you are or what title you have. Nobody in Silicon Valley could in his or her wildest dreams imagine that the next big thing will come from a Senior Vice President; it is far more likely to come from a newly hired 21-year-old. As we have seen, in this collaborative model the relevant adage is no longer "Knowledge is power", but "Knowledge sharing is power".

A valuable challenge is to turn tacit knowledge into explicit knowledge. You need to orchestrate the knowledge in your organization. Thoughts that are not written down or documented are pure vaporware. I believe in documenting thoughts and knowledge in writing – it gives clarity of mind. Knowledge is to be found in the tension between the organization and the individual. The more decentralized a corporation is, the more important it becomes to gather knowledge centrally in order to ensure collective learning. The complexity of the data increases steadily and as a result, so does the need for insight. We all share the task of documenting tacit knowledge and reducing the dependence upon specific individuals in order to strengthen the corporation.

Knowledge sharing is central to the process. Knowledge sharing enables you to become dispensable and allows you to throw yourself into new challenges, giving you even more knowledge which you, in turn, can share. My experience is that the more you give the more you get. It is difficult to overestimate the joy and the pride of giving. But it is one thing to have the information – something else to have it formatted into knowledge. Performance management is the discipline that specifies and generates optimal management reporting. The management group is dependent on the right reports – but often the aggregation level is so high that it becomes difficult to see and interpret the key ratios. Therefore it is important, from time to time, to seek knowledge directly at source so that you are able to challenge causalities, support hypotheses and obtain spontaneous answers. This process of documenting knowledge is central to the activity advocated in this book; if you've been acting on the exercises presented here, developing your own Personal Business Plan, then you are documenting your knowledge and making tacit assumptions, intentions and aspirations explicit.

Consultative value is created by an agenda directed at clarifying interpersonal interactions and focusing on relational and emotional dynamics. You can train laser-sharp attention on the organizational dimensions that are usually overlooked, disparaged, illegitimate, avoided, and unconscious, or taken for granted. This includes a wide spectrum of issues varying from political agendas, internal competition, power plays, conventional, and fixed preconceptions of roles and expectations – to paradigms about the leader's real ability to predict, control, make rational choices, and cope with reality. Some progressive companies, such as Cisco, go even further. They expect and encourage leaders and employees to disrupt business as usual in order to exploit future potentials.

Let's now think about those in conventional consultant roles. When at their best:

- The academic presents theories which lead to new ways of understanding and putting into perspective both the world and the role of leadership.
- The management consultant participates in a concrete business initiative where she, together with the client organization, creates a common project where her outsider perspective fertilizes insider knowledge and leads to new understandings – supported by various tools, concepts, and analytical and relational competencies.
- The coach creates a reflective space where the participants become aware of their own experience patterns and are supported in creating a new meaning, and developing their thinking and practice.
- The process consultant works alongside a leadership team and, in contrast to the individual coach, has access to more views of reality, and may facilitate spontaneous relational shifts in understanding and practice of the participants.

Inspiration: Express Your Feelings

Neurologically speaking, intelligent function evolves to keep control of emotional impulses. If you don't keep these impulses under some kind of control, your mind is hijacked and you feel at the mercy of emotional blackmail. Howard Gardner defines Emotional Competence as:[110]

- Self-awareness (to know one's emotions).
- Self-control (to control one's emotions).
- Self-motivation (to motivate oneself).
- Empathy (to recognize emotions in others).
- Sense of occasion (to deal with others).

It is precisely when it is extremely difficult to articulate an emotion that it is most important do so. Many of us have grown up in a conflict adverse environment where you simply have to get along. As a consequence we learn to suppress negative feelings – but they are still there. When we have difficulty expressing a feeling it is probably because it is in conflict with some of our fundamental beliefs.

We hang on to our downloading paradigm in order to protect ourselves, so one of your fundamental challenges is to push the barriers for what is perceived as dangerous or threatening. Ask the obvious question. It is fine to assert yourself – an assertive attitude will increase your circle of influence. What doesn't kill you will make you stronger!

The good consultant, often through an eclectic and flexible approach, points at signals which were previously neglected. You already knew of their existence, but you simply had not yet communicated the messages clearly to yourself. The aim then is to crystallize and synthesize common knowledge and radically formulate simplicity that lies beyond complexity.

What is My BATNA?

Sometimes challenges are as confusing as trying to repair and maintain the plane while it is in the air. So you need to simplify, and that is what BATNA does for you – your *Best Alternative to Negotiated Agreement*. The BATNA concept was developed as part of The Harvard Negotiation Project which developed the Interest Based Negotiation technique.[111]

Two of the key principles are:

⊗ Separate the people from the problem.
⊗ Focus on interests, not positions.

There is power in understanding interests and there is power in developing a good BATNA. The value of stating your interests precisely cannot be overestimated; being able to identify priorities and document them is key to opening up the possibility of solving challenges in a generous and mutually beneficial way. Looking at your future, your BATNA gives you a benchmark against which you can measure any future situation compared to your current situation. It protects you from:

- ⬦ Accepting terms that are too unfavorable
- ⬦ Rejecting terms that would be in your interest to accept

When developing your BATNA, you may want to consider the different risk elements of a simple projection of your present work and lifestyle. If this realistic projection does not seem appealing for some reason, then it is time to change. Remember your personal 20/20 Vision: "What goals can I possibly devise that will make me learn and grow as much or more in the next 20 years as I have learnt and grown for the last 20 years?"

When planning your future you should keep a few principles in mind:

- ⬦ Protect the downside – How do I exit?
- ⬦ Never bite the hand that feeds you.
- ⬦ Never wound a king.
- ⬦ Hit the ground running – get traction from the start.

Sometimes it may also help to follow the advice of Richard Branson: "Screw it – let's do it". In *Business Stripped Bare*, Richard Branson describes his phenomenal rise to the top.[112] Looking behind the narrative, there is no doubt that Richard Branson is positively addicted. Psychologically, he is addicted to the rush it gives to create and get attention. As he gets results, his level of ambition rises and he needs to continuously develop his business and himself. His positive addiction also makes him a more open, visionary, and altruistic person. Again, one of the reasons for Branson's success is a well-developed self-discipline.

Sometimes you just create your own possibilities as you go along and new opportunities arise out of the blue. You realize that you are standing on the shoulders of giants and help materializes. When you stop downloading, you become inspired and ideas and initiatives develop spontaneously and you are able to create the new and different. The challenge is to dare to dare.

Am I Happy Now?

> **❝** Learn from Yesterday.
> Live for Today and
> Hope for Tomorrow **❞**
> *Albert Einstein*

A former colleague once stopped me at the train station and said: "You look good. Are you also well?" That left me puzzled. In Claus Otto Scharmer's terms it was a mixture of two elements from the downloading and the dialogue universe, respectively. It simply left me there on the platform thinking: We shouldn't take ourselves too seriously.

So how are you right now? The tough reality you have to face up to is that if you are not happy now, you will never be happy! The American essayist Agnes Repplier wrote: "It is not easy to find happiness within ourselves, and it is impossible to find it elsewhere". This reality makes the need to become happy somewhat urgent! In order to achieve this, you must dare to be yourself – it is fundamental to the quality of your leadership. A part of your developmental process is to find your inner greatness. Be respected for who you are and not what you are. Show tolerance and respect, inclusiveness and diversity, flexibility and integrity. Live and let live.

The ideal life is not free of challenges – you need to find the patterns in your life that are counterproductive and then change them. Sometimes it means satisfying instead of optimizing – remove the stone in your shoe. Solve your problems from the solution side – don't dwell on the problem itself. Confront issues from a future perspective. Create your own reality. Goals are dreams with deadlines. The meaning of life is to find a goal that you are willing to die for.

Inspiration: The Top Five Regrets of the Dying

Recently I fell over proof of the value of maintaining the big perspective; an incredible demonstration of the importance of meaningfulness. Bronnie Ware is an Australian nurse, who for years worked in a hospice taking care of dying people. She wrote a book *The Top Five Regrets of the Dying*[113] about the thoughts that we have at the end of life. Bronnie Ware notes that all her patients found a form of inner peace before the curtain fell. But especially five regrets emerged over and over again in her talks with those whose life was about to end. They wished . . .

1. That they had been happier. That they more often had broken the monotony and done all these things that they knew made them happy.
2. That they had worked less. Especially the male patients would spend more time with their family if they could redo their life.
3. That they had been more honest. That they more often had expressed their feelings instead of suppressing them.
4. That they had cared more about their friendships. Too many had thoughtlessly lost contact with people they loved to be with.
5. The fifth and last message Bronnie Ware heard was also the most common. This is the way she quotes her patients: *"I wish I had had the courage to live a life which was true to myself instead of the life that others expected of me."*

Then she adds:

" This was the most common regret of all. When people realize that their life is nearly over and they look back with clarity it becomes obvious how many dreams were not fulfilled. Most had not even honored half of their dreams and they had to die being conscious that this was due to the choices that they had made or not made. *"*

The concept of meaningfulness is about themes that give you personal meaning in life so that you feel that it's worth investing energy, engagement, and commitment. If you have a strong sense of meaningfulness, you often talk in an engaged way about all the areas in your life which mean a lot to you. If you have a weak sense of meaningfulness you rarely express that anything in life has any particular importance. This doesn't mean that individuals with a strong sense of meaningfulness feel happy when a relative dies or a war breaks out – but rather that they face the challenge with a fixed determination to create personal meaning in what happens. One way to avoid being hit or hurt by rapid change is to create personal meaning. Your personal principles show the way and give a feeling of direction, even in a time characterized by turbulence. You experience living as a challenge – rather than as a burden you would rather be without – precisely because it gives personal, emotional, and private meaning.

Flemming's Tale: Inspired to Be at His Best

Flemming completed his Personal Business Plan over a period of 12 months during which we carried out ten Executive Coaching sessions – each covering one of the book chapters. They were all sessions filled with energy and joy – a true spirit of rejuvenation and lightheartedness. Although existential in nature, the questions inspired and motivated Flemming to be at his best – aspiring for an ambitious dream that he would never have been able to formulate on his own – let alone building the courage to actually act and live out the dream. As mentioned several times a fundamental prerequisite for success in life is to have the courage to commit yourself. Flemming definitely felt happy and at ease. He was eager to take on new challenges and prove himself by stepping up to a higher level. And most of all, he was able to do it by himself, not being dependent of others. It was his choice, his commitment, and his personal success criterion. He was ready.

Jan's Tale: A New and Improved Version of Himself

Jan also followed a program consisting of ten Executive Coaching sessions over a period of 12 months. As his Personal Business Plan clearly shows, he had become a new and improved version of himself. He was now much more conscious of the effect he had on others, as well as the levers he could use in order to maximize his impact. He had strengthened some of his beneficial behavior and damage controlled on some of the behavior which didn't create value for him. Jan felt optimistic, self-confident and even more as a leader. He had obtained clarity and couldn't wait to execute his plan.

Key Learning

- Your vision of where or who you want to be is the greatest asset you have.
- Give yourself some spin. Don't give a speech. Put on a show.
- Create and contribute to networks – it will reduce friction for you.
- Reduce nervous energy by balancing your hectic lifestyle with deliberation.
- Find value in what you do, and identify your specific and unique contribution.
- Sharpen your emotional intelligence by addressing issues assertively.
- Identify your BATNA – your Best Alternative to Negotiated Agreement.
- Sometimes positive addiction is good. As you get results, your level of ambition and your need to continuously develop yourself rises.
- If you are not happy now, you will never be happy.
- The meaning of life is to find a goal that you are willing to die for.

10

What Have I Learned?

*// The best time to plant a tree is twenty years ago.
The second best time is today //*
Chinese proverb

I now have a very simple – albeit demanding exercise for you.

It would be very beneficial for you if you could synthesize your specific needs. Very often, when working with leaders over a longer period of time, it is at this junction that they see the light. They came to me with one or two questions on their mind – now they see some existential themes emerge.

Inspiration: Your Existential Themes

I would like you to go through the chapters again and from the whole book identify three key learning themes that apply to you – and then implement them without further discussion.

Theme 1:

Theme 2:

Theme 3:

If you haven't already done so, it is also time to construct your own Four-Leaf Clover. The most differentiating dimension is the pivotal concept at the center of the leaves. Some of the potential candidates for central concepts, that we have discussed, are *Happiness, Leadership*, and *Reinvention*. Another potential candidate could be *Personal Development*. It's important that you define the themes in your life. Refer back to Chapter 7 *How Do I Reinvent Myself?* if you need to.

As a source of inspiration you may want to revisit my examples of Four-Leaf Clovers in Figure 1, page ix and Figure 17, page 113. Your aim is to synthesize the existential themes that have emerged in your life. It is a question of defining the cross-fertilization that will create the most value for you. In practice this is done by playing with different alternatives until all of a sudden you get an impression of clarity and connectedness. This moment of truth will occur – don't worry!

Figure 20 Your Four-Leaf Clover

Flemming's Four-Leaf Clover looks like this:

ART AND ARCHITECTURE

博思明 Bo Si Ming
(Profound Bright Thinking)

CATALYTIC SOCIETY

ENTREPRENEUR

DIGNITY

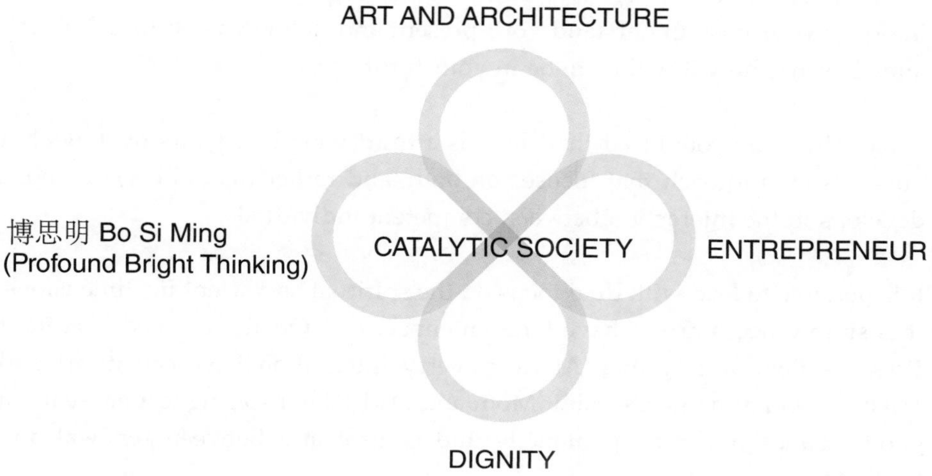

Figure 21 Flemming's Four-Leaf Clover

Jan's Four-Leaf Clover looks like this:

FATHER

LEADER

A LIFE WELL LIVED

BUSINESSMAN

ADVENTURER

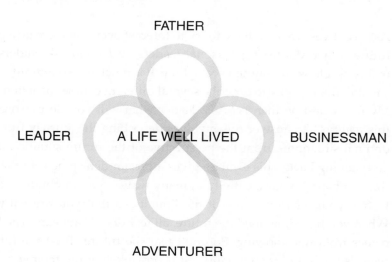

Figure 22 Jan's Four-Leaf Clover

Now it's all about you. You need to be convinced about yourself in order to be convincing. Trust from others is earned through self-confidence.[114] You must believe in what you are doing and, in order to do this, you need to have had a moment of revelation where you have clearly experienced your own future.

Your four-leaf clover will enable you to live the life you want to live. Your reawakened sense of purpose is an overpowering force. You are now able to interpret your past, understand your present and define your future. You can already sense how it will be to be in your future.

Personally, I am convinced that there is a third way: Not yours or mine, but ours. It's an approach that focuses on both/and rather than either/or, and it develops in the interaction between competent individuals.

It is possible to lead with dual focus on the spiritual and scientific dimensions. It is simply necessary to have long antennae. In L'Oréal we called it *Poête et Paysan* – Poet and Farmer. At Korn/Ferry International we call it Art and Science – and at home we call it Mom and Dad! The inspiring leader creates a good balance between spontaneity and control and between renewal and tradition.

What is My Time Horizon?

As executives we often have to try to forecast events and create a picture of the future. When discussing personal leadership I often ask leaders to describe reality as it looks in, say, ten years' time. It is much more committing to describe a reality than merely to describe several different courses of action or scenarios. My next question then is "As a leader what will you do personally to create this reality?" To answer this involves describing the journey from now to the optimal situation – from the perspective of the future situation and meaning and looking back. This exercise gives a certain detachment to the process and this can benefit your creativity in many ways – you might, for example, want to free yourself from some of the limitations that you presently experience. When you have imagined the future, all fear of it disappears. The fear, after all, comes from not knowing. So don't fear the future. Trust the future. In most regards life is a plus sum game – it is possible to grow the pie.

Portraits of top executives in the media may sometimes give the reader the impression that the chief executive is a commander, or even a king, rather than a manager, and that the organization is an army or a kingdom. As mentioned in Blue Ocean Strategy,[115] strategy language is permeated with military references – we talk about a corporation's "headquarters", about "the troops", and about "the front line". A strategy that is expressed in such a way implies that we are confronting an adversary and fighting over a given area of land which is limited and constant – in other words a zero sum game. It does not give any leverage and does not multiply value. I believe in collaboration and the power of the network which could lead to the following definition of synergy: $2 + 2 =$ The Beatles.

How Far Can I Go?

Your biological success criterion is to live as long as possible. Therefore you need to take care of yourself and this means both your mind and your body. Meditation is a technique that could help you attain a state of relaxed readiness, and physical exercise will help you build and maintain your energy reserves. In today's hectic environment it is simply necessary from time to time to change the context, relax, and recharge the batteries.

When you meditate or concentrate, you find lots of useless thoughts: Opinions which were once valid but long ago lost their significance. Now they simply take up mental space and block new creative thoughts. To process former negative and positive experiences gives you a fresh, pure glimpse of the now. In practice meditation is just a period of reflection; when you meditate you prepare yourself for whatever may come – you clear the noise. Very often it becomes clear that the potential conflict or dilemma which you have struggled with only existed in your imagination.

Rational arguments tend to reinforce duality and our own limited viewpoint. By slowing down you are often able to transform a conflict into an opportunity to radically improve a relationship.

An amazing number of the successful leaders I have talked to share similar rituals. They focus their attention on the critical issues, very often by meditative or reflective rituals in the early morning. If you spend half an hour alone with yourself every morning contemplating the complexity of the tasks at hand, you will experience a feeling of clarity and peacefulness which will remain with you for the rest of the day. The discipline of this process of clarification will render you more robust during the day – it will enable you to continue giving without becoming emotionally drained. In short, the function of a ritual is to leverage the quality of a relationship. This can be the relationship to an object, to your work, to your deeper self or to other people. Think leverage: Define your personal contribution and identify your key value proposition. The Greek philosopher and physicist Archimedes put it in the following way: "Give me a long enough lever and a place to stand, and I can move the World."

Attention is of primordial importance in modern leadership – attention towards yourself and towards your surroundings. Concentration is the most important method of improving attention and once you have done this, you are able to think what you want to think and, hence, do what you want to do. The answer to "What?" is the decision. The answer to "How?" is the execution.

In order to capitalize on new opportunities you need to act with non-conformity as your guideline and, in doing this, become a change agent. The greater the number of people who agree on a solution, the greater the risk that it is a conventional solution. Therefore always seek unconventional wisdom. This reminds me of a leadership development activity in which I once participated. Directions were given for a complex treasure hunt and the teams all rushed off to find the prize. There was an old man standing by the side of the road, but none of the teams took the time to stop and ask the old man for advice. It turned out that the old man had the unconventional key to solve the problem. Since then I have tried to always ask the old man!

We are our own hardest judge and drill sergeant – I have seen many entrepreneurs seeking freedom and flexibility, and ending up with more work than they ever imagined. Winners tend to have a Plan B. Never enter a business without knowing how to get out: Always have an exit strategy. That also goes for your life.

What Would I Attempt to Do if I Knew I Could Not Fail?

Try to govern your life by going forward under this principle. It speaks to big dreams, innovation, personal challenge, and pushing to create what is next. Free yourself from the limitations created by your past. Look to the future and the best possible opportunity. Most analytical tools will simply help you extrapolate your past – this is not necessarily gratifying. You must create personal breakthroughs which bring you closer to your optimal Self. By all means identify which events brought you here, but consider your past experiences as building blocks for your future – how can you use them in the best possible way? Disregard some of the advice given to you earlier on – you have probably already evolved so significantly that the advice is no longer relevant – you have probably already compensated for any potential weaknesses and corrected the course. I have interviewed so many candidates who claim they are shy or reticent but, if they had not told me, I would not have noticed. Often this introversion stems from their childhood and, in the meantime, they have developed into professional extroverts. The only limiting factor is in their heads!

If entrepreneurs didn't believe in themselves, they would never embark on the journey. Rationally, their actions are against all odds. They bet on creating something original in a world with seven billion brains. Therefore, faith always plays a role. I haven't written much about faith in this book but it is essential for your success that you believe in the messages that you tell yourself and others.

When you have created Your Personal Business Plan, which is meaningful to you, you are free to run with it. You will never become faster or more agile than you are just now. Everything is open. It is easy to find out whether you have reached your goal. When you are able to read your Personal Business Plan without being scared by the future, you believe in the project. You must feel a strong emotional bond with your goal – then you become your goal.

The startup analogy can be useful in many ways. A very tangible tool is the concept of *pivot or persevere* which is described by Eric Ries in his book *The Lean Startup*[116]. The thinking behind this dictates that you as an entrepreneur sooner or later will meet a fundamental dilemma: Should you stick to your strategy – or should you rethink it in the light of your experience and the adversity that you meet? I like the word pivot. When you pivot, you turn on yourself, typically keeping one foot to the ground. Literally, you maintain a fulcrum even if you end up having turned 180 degrees.

According to Eric Ries many entrepreneurs who adapt their strategy say that they wish they had done it earlier. This entirely matches my experience. People regret what they didn't do, not what they did. One of the most common comments I get from senior executives is that they gave too long a leash to low performers. They found different excuses for keeping people on board even though results were lacking. So one key learning for you is, *if it doesn't work, then fix it now*! The concept of *pivot or persevere* can be a valuable tool in your personal development. When you feel the need to adjust the strategy you must figuratively look for the foot that you will leave on the ground, corresponding to the elements of Your Personal Business Plan that you will stick to. Then you can adapt your strategy and your future plans without giving up the plan in its entirety. Sometimes it is only possible to have a three-month road map. Most often you will choose to carry over your life ambition, your key competencies and your functional conditions.

Before was the past. Now is happiness. After is the future. The past is the past, look to the future. Move on; maintain the momentum and get the best out of your past. Find out for yourself that there are no true answers; you must create your own. Don't think that your opinions and points of view are unchangeable; kill your darlings. Reinvent yourself – this will give you a second wind. Fantasy and the power of imagination is a marvelous driver of creation. So free yourself from conventional thinking, see through conventional wisdom, and challenge the norms. Whereas knowledge is something you can obtain from others, wisdom you must experience and gain for yourself. Look through the charade and choose your own path. Rituals help in making the difficult simple. Don't forget to ask the important and underlying question "Why?" Why am I doing what I do? Who am I trying to satisfy?

Albert Einstein said: "There is nothing that is a more certain sign of insanity than to do the same thing over and over and expect the results to be different".

A top executive must explicitly embrace his or her positions, opinions, and values, and communicate them clearly. The communication must be relevant, meaning messages that are translated into the perspective of the receiver and which the top executive personally and wholeheartedly can vouch for.

I sometimes think of myself as Personal Content Provider as I truly believe that "Content is King". Communication is what is being heard: Language is the content. Ludwig Wittgenstein puts it the following way: "The limits of my language are the limits of my world". I have always been fascinated by such iconic statements as Martin Luther King's "I have a dream" and Kennedy's "Ich bin ein Berliner" or Obama's "Yes, we can". I shiver when I hear such condensed meaning. However, the source of your personal meaning is to be found within you, not in external factors.

Professor Ralph Stacey, in his Gesture–Response theory, goes deeper into the importance of our understanding of relationships.[117] We may control the gesture that we send but not the response we receive. Command and control does not belong in modern business life. As leaders, the only thing we can do is to increase the probability of receiving the desired response and this is done through relationships. A much sought after key competency is the ability to see around corners, to increase the probability of a certain response. Sometimes, however, a "black swan" occurs. A "black swan" represents an event with great impact which seldom occurs and which lies beyond what one would normally expect. When events such as the September 11, 2011 attack on Twin Towers or the 2004 Indian Ocean tsunami occur, you get a feeling of being lost in the matrix. Such rare and unanticipated events destabilize your radar by rocking your value system. However, the success and speed of your response to a "black swan" event is intimately related to your sense of personal meaning and purpose. If your sense of yourself is firm, you will better resist the buffering of unexpected events and more effectively recover your control over proceedings.

When you have created your quintessential goals, then stick to them. When you have chosen the things in your life that you are willing to fight for, then go for them. Sometimes you need to strengthen your distinctiveness and uniqueness in order to cut through the wall of noise that surrounds you. Abraham Lincoln said that "Every man is born an original, but sadly, most men die as copies". The most interesting and challenging people I have met have kept their freshness against all odds. They are still fighting for their ideas and are still originals. They probably have their own Personal Business Plan.

Flemming's Tale: What Did He Learn?

Reminiscing on his Executive Coaching process, some of Flemming's concluding remarks were the following. He had striven for clarity of thought and decisiveness of mind. He had not been afraid of existential thoughts – trusting that they were there to protect him in the long run. He perceived himself as excellent – and he had not been afraid of ridicule. He had been as pragmatic in planning his life as he had been in planning a project – realizing that his life was the ultimate project. Flemming had chosen to say no to things that he didn't enjoy. He had learnt to listen to his own needs instead of the expectations of others. He had consciously transferred relationships and contact persons from Realdania to Flemming. He had also really understood that when leaving Realdania and starting his new life, his obligations towards Realdania and colleagues ceased to exist. He deeply felt that here were no strings to tie him down. He had found that in life the best way to learn is through action. The journey had taught him all he needed to know.

Jan's Tale: What Did He Learn?

Looking back at his Executive Coaching process, Jan defined the following concluding house rules for himself: Your work is a way of financing your life. You need to have fun at your work. It's all about the courage to pursue your dreams. Be loyal – but not stupid. Be honest and trustworthy. Conserve your childish soul. You can only live your own life. The vision is often worth more than the realization. Keep your empathy and dedication in everything you do. Remember to enjoy life.

Jan had definitely experienced some deep insights and had the courage to act upon them. From thinking to doing!

As Flemming's and Jan's tales have clearly shown – and as you have no doubt personally experienced through your own work with your Personal Business Plan – it is a very versatile and flexible framework. It gives you robust, rewarding and long-lasting benefits. There are no rights or wrongs. The crucial thing is to choose your own life ambition and relentlessly, albeit lightheartedly, follow it through. I would like to illustrate this point by quoting one happy executive:

" After having gone through this program, I thought of a way of visualizing the seismic change that had taken place inside of me. I imagined that I met myself the way I was one year ago. That person wouldn't stand a chance compared to me today! *"*

Key Learning

- Define your three key learning themes and implement them – now.
- Be sure to convince yourself before convincing others.
- What will you do now to personally create your ideal future?
- When you have imagined your future, all fear of it disappears.
- Your biological success criterion is to live as long as possible – so take care.
- Clean out your mental attic.
- Slow down to speed up.
- Concentrate on your main value proposition and simplify radically.
- Fight for your ideas.
- What would you attempt to do if you knew you could not fail?

EPILOGUE: WHAT NOW?

> *" The biggest failure is having success*
> *– and not being happy "*
> *Anthony Robbins*

Since the 1990s, every summer I have participated at the week-long Roskilde Rock Festival in Denmark. I have noticed that as soon as I start talking about the festival my voice changes. I am simply thrilled by live concerts – they give me energy. Together with the 100 000 other festival goers I am automatically in the sensing position. Some things at the festival are unchanged since my first visit in the 1970s. I have had my base in the same camp since 1995. Other things are continuously changing. Many of the norms of society are temporarily suspended and in the tolerant and inclusive atmosphere of the festival new surprises wait around every tent corner. Roskilde Festival calls itself a boundary-pushing cultural-political manifestation – and it can't be put more precisely than that. Their codex for the camp area goes like this:

> *" Share*, what you have, without expecting the least in return. Have nearly naïve *trust* that others wish you the best. Lean forward and *participate*. Keep your eyes *open* and your mind *free*. Cherish *playing*, and invite others – not only those who you know. *Surprise* yourself. Meet challenges on your way with a *hug* and a *smile*. *"*

That is charming, isn't it?

In front of the stages I am together with people I would never normally meet in other contexts. The diversity is extraordinary. So what is the link between a rock festival and executive coaching and executive search? The annual festival is a way for me to move out of my comfort zone and into a new and different universe which gives me a totally different perspective than the white walls in my elegant office. It forces me out of stereotypical thinking and routine acting. It sharpens my curiosity. In other words the festival helps in keeping me mentally young, which is totally aligned with my life ambition.

I trust that, through Your work with Your Personal Business Plan, you have reached a higher level of self-awareness. Aligning your life with a greater perspective gives a certain peace of mind. This will naturally lead you on the path of generosity: Giving while living.

In parallel with finishing this book I read *Rework* by Jason Fried and David Heinemeier Hansson.[118] It is an explosion of good advice for entrepreneurs. Everything in the book focuses on companies: How to think of them, how to manage them and develop them, how to man them. *Rework*'s authors provokingly and intelligently describe how many cemented perceptions are breaking up. The old management thinking – streamlined and boxed-in, as it was – doesn't fit the conditions of the new time any longer.

In the digital age the success criterion is getting your product out in the market as soon as possible. You're an idiot if you release your first version without errors. In the new world, entrepreneurs talk about the *Minimum Viable Product* – the *least* finished product you can allow yourself to throw on the market. This would have been heresy in the old industrial paradigm. When I worked with L'Oréal and The Coca-Cola Company, we analyzed and pre-tested every detail before launching any product. Today many new companies present their product to the market – and then they progressively turn up perfection as they get feedback from customers. And here's the point. *You are your own startup.*

Rework's representation of modern entrepreneurship could equally describe how you obtain success in your career. Consider yourself as having decoded your self-limitations and as having one fundamental idea. That you give up the old and take a chance on the conditions of the future. Of course the market might reveal that you need to adapt your idea, that you must redirect – but you are on your way.

Many people think about starting their own company, but don't because of the risk. In the planning of your career you must jump into things just as the entrepreneurs – and with the same energy. I know many entrepreneurs and they all have momentum, they look out of the window and see opportunities, opportunities, and opportunities. You should aim to have the same ingenuity and creative urge. Then you will be able to make decisions without hesitation – decisions that will move as pebbles going down a hillside – when the movement has started, it is unstoppable. Just do it.

When you reach the mental state of the entrepreneur you start thinking more freely. What fascinates me about entrepreneurs is that they are not limited by the past. The day their company is born there is no "before". There is only the intensity of the present and the promise of the future. Real entrepreneurs often have an artistic or creative vein that makes them appreciate the performance in making something new. They don't chase recognition and status, deep down they believe in the end product. Of course there is always a financial perspective but in the entrepreneur's radiation the core is more of a love story.

Your life ambition is probably the strongest tool that you take with you from this book. You will experience the power of the life ambition concept by turning theory into action – and action into value for you. Behavior follows reward. It is no coincidence that one of the words that I have used many times in this book is "behavior". Your strength lies in your actions – your audiences are not mind readers – they will only react to what they see – what you do. Never forget the origin of the word responsibility: *response ability*. It's all up to you.

With this in mind please take a few minutes to read and think through the following pieces of good advice that I have collected from different Personal Business Plans developed by numerous executives, whom I have had the privilege to coach. Select the two or three themes that provide you with a sensation of stretch – that provoke you to maintain a life ambitious attitude.

- Start young.
- "Frontload" has always been one of my mantras: Why wait if it's possible to do it now? Don't waste time unnecessarily. Don't procrastinate.
- Stay fit.
- Do whatever is necessary in order to exercise your body. You will be more stress-resistant and robust.

♲ Practice endurance.

♲ Don't quit. Life is a marathon – or at least a relay. You become better and better when exploring your own frontiers.

♲ Work hard.

♲ It is necessary to fight for what you believe in. And that might just mean that you will actually sweat. So be it.

♲ Don't go straight, go forwards.

♲ Be sure that every step you take moves you in the right direction. Sometimes it is necessary to digress in order to escape obstacles.

♲ Make things happen.

♲ Act. Don't wait for the perfect circumstances to arise. They never will. However, if you are decisive you will be able to seize the optimal moment.

♲ Trust your instinct.

♲ Follow your first impulse. Most often – just like in Trivial Pursuit – it is the right answer or association that pops up. Sometimes we tend to rationalize the right answer away.

♲ Love yourself.

♲ Be proud of who you are and what you have done. If you don't love yourself you make it harder for others to love you.

♲ Don't let the past limit you.

♲ The past has left a significant imprint on who you are. Look at your future potential rather than your past limitations.

♲ Be ambitious.

♲ Go for it. Raise the bar. Don't hesitate at formulating extremely challenging goals. Then it will be so much more fun reaching them.

♲ Anticipate. Think ahead. Have a Plan B.

♲ Be free of guilt.

♲ You live your life. Others live their lives. It is not your responsibility how they choose to live their lives. Act with self-interest in mind – while still being merciful.

♲ Take time to reflect.

♲ Stop the hamster wheel from time to time. Pause and think about your direction. If you were to die tomorrow, would this be your preferred way of spending your last day?

♲ Stretch yourself.

♲ Don't go for the path with the least resistance. Be brave and go for challenge that builds character. Crave for excitement and the unexpected.

♲ Be happy.

- ✧ Remember to enjoy the ride. There are always lots of reasons to postpone celebrating and being thankful. Sometimes it's enough simply enjoying the now.
- ✧ Have the courage to commit yourself.
- ✧ Last but not least throw yourself into the unknown. Choose your life partner without waiting eternally for the perfect one. Choose a good job without waiting eternally for the perfect one. Choose a good house or apartment without waiting eternally for the perfect one. Make them the perfect ones.

I trust that Your Personal Business Plan has made you happier.

Go to bed with a dream, wake up with a purpose.

To infinity . . . and beyond!

YOUR PERSONAL BUSINESS PLAN TOOLKIT

It is important that the well-documented and time-tested framework of *The Personal Business Plan* leads to action for you and makes you succeed in your endeavors, just as it has for so many other life ambitious individuals. The following Toolkit gives you a template from which to answer all the key questions that you have been given to think about over the course of reading the book. You will also find this Toolkit available to download at thepersonalbusinessplan.com.

1 What is My Situation?

If you have difficulties in defining this, take your immediate answers to the following three questions. Then ask yourself the most simple and effective follow-up question of our language: "Why?"

Write down your answers in the spaces provided below.

What baggage of the past must I let go of?

What is meaningful to me right now?
To this end you may also ask yourself: "What preoccupies me?" and "What are my stay-awake issues?"

How can I move forward?

2 How Can I Thrive?

Wellbeing Analysis (Heaven and Hell):

Draw a horizontal line which represents your lifespan – along this line, plot in all the major events of your life. In a vertical axis on the left, plot in your wellbeing at the different events in your life. If it's positive (*Heaven*), you plot it above the horizontal line, if it's negative (*Hell*), your plot it below.

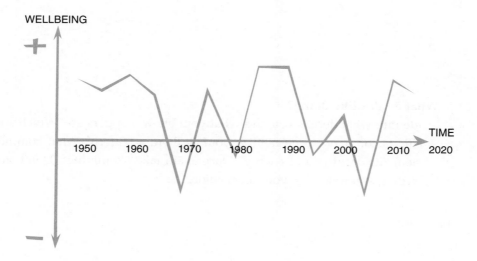

Also, go to thepersonalbusinessplan.com *for an interactive version of this tool.*

What do I like doing?

Take 6½ minutes to write down what you like doing. You must write without interruption. Associations will follow freely. Don't stop writing. You can do it. Now!

What don't I like doing?

Identify what derails you and what your show stoppers are. Which specific factors tend to destabilize you? Is there a pattern? What common elements drain you of energy? Once again take 6½ minutes. Don't stop writing and follow all your associations.

How can I learn to trust my intuition?

3 When Do I Perform at My Best?

What does success look like to me?

Functional Conditions	First job 19ab–19cd	Second job 19cd–19ef	Third job 19ef–19gh	Fourth job 19gh–20ij	Fifth job 20ij–20kl	Present job 20kl–Now

Use the table to rate each of your positions for each of the characteristics. 1 = positive, 2 = neutral and 3 = negative. Think of it as awarding them a Gold (1), Silver (2) or Bronze (3) medal.

What is my deep-down motivation?

Start with questions like: Why do I do what I do? Why do I take the chances that I do? What would make me happy? What keeps me from achieving this? When do I feel at my best? When do I find my work most fun? What have I ever developed a passionate interest in? What would make a difference in my perceived quality of life? What difference would I like to have made, when I look back on my life?

What is my worst-case scenario?

Remember, the worst outcome is seldom as bad as you fear, so take a risk!

4 What Energizes Me?

What are my strengths?

Reflect on when the three following concepts have been in harmony with each other: Your personal values; Your competencies; The tasks that you solve:

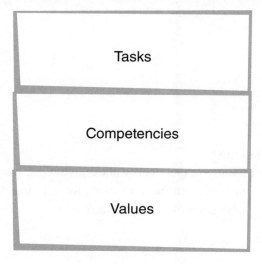

What are my weaknesses?

Now document your strengths and weaknesses and identify where associated opportunities and threats lie. Be wary of strengths that may conceal future threats and pay particular attention to signature strengths that can be turned into existential opportunities. A general guideline is: Focus on your strengths and damage control on your weaknesses.

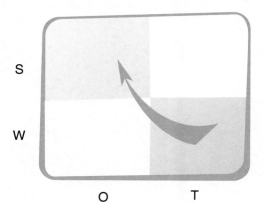

Strengths

Weaknesses

Opportunities

Threats

What is my passion?
Think about what you feel deeply about, what excites you, and what you would do if you did not have to work for a living. Could you make a career and a living out of your passion?

5 Where am I on My Personal Journey?

Where am I in my life?

Ask yourself: "In which life phase am I? And what's the next? And the next?"

What are my personal priorities?

Be honest with yourself and focus on how you can realign your life to work towards the results you want.

What is my potential for personal growth?

Exploit opportunities by identifying new challenges. Take responsibility for your mood and your behavior, create moments of joy and give time for reflection.

6 How Do I Become Happy?

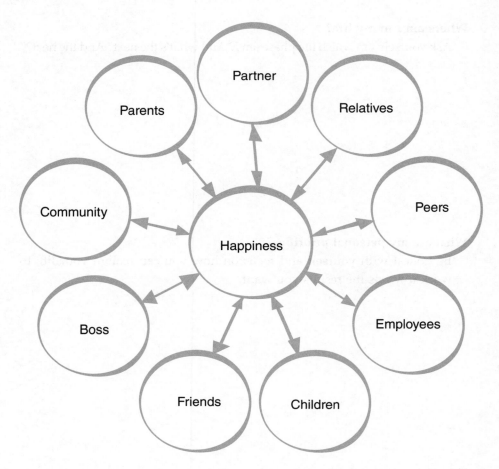

What is my challenge?

Think about your current situation? Where do you want to make changes in order to improve your state of mind and feeling of happiness?

Why must I do something now?

What is causing you frustration? Are you lacking some satisfaction in your daily life? Think about why you simply cannot let things go on as they are.

How can I obtain 20/20 vision?

Focus on your learning curve for the last 20 years. Identify the events or actions that triggered the most learning and personal growth. When and why did you grow most? Now look at this shaded area for the last 20 years – your challenge is to ensure that the shaded area under the curve for the next 20 years is at least as big. So what goals can you possibly invent that are challenging enough to live up to this tough demand?

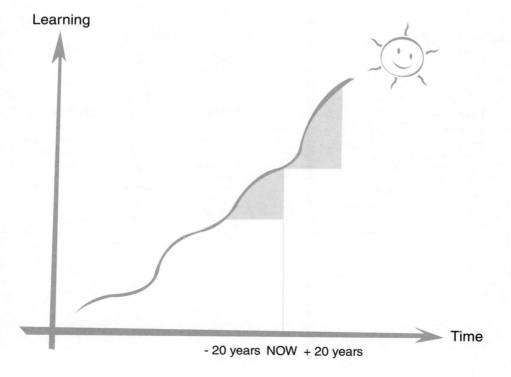

7 How Do I Reinvent Myself?

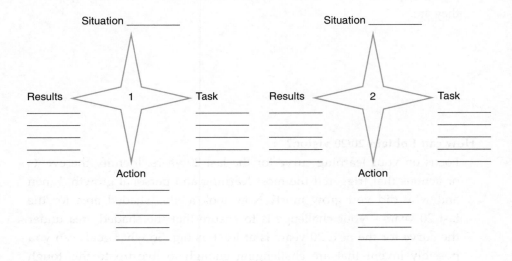

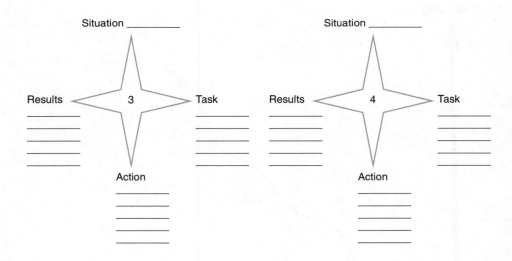

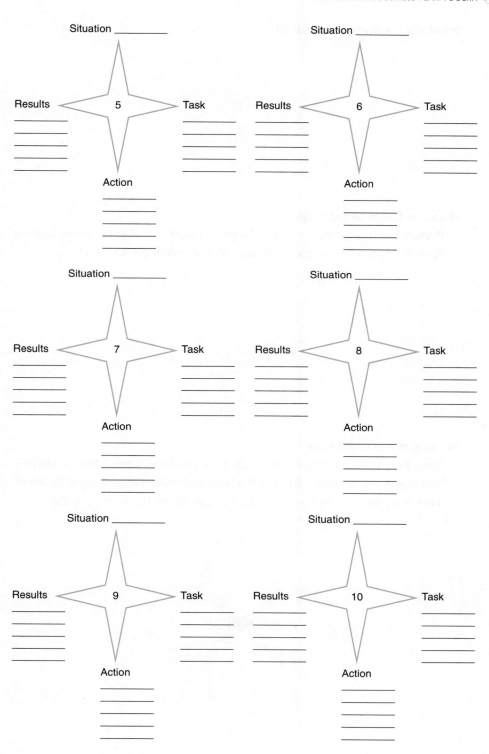

Situation _____

Results   5   Task
_____   _____
_____   _____
_____   _____
_____   _____
_____

        Action
        _____
        _____
        _____
        _____

Situation _____

Results   6   Task
_____   _____
_____   _____
_____   _____
_____   _____

        Action
        _____
        _____
        _____
        _____

Situation _____

Results   7   Task
_____   _____
_____   _____
_____   _____
_____   _____

        Action
        _____
        _____
        _____
        _____

Situation _____

Results   8   Task
_____   _____
_____   _____
_____   _____
_____   _____

        Action
        _____
        _____
        _____
        _____

Situation _____

Results   9   Task
_____   _____
_____   _____
_____   _____
_____   _____

        Action
        _____
        _____
        _____
        _____

Situation _____

Results   10   Task
_____   _____
_____   _____
_____   _____
_____   _____

        Action
        _____
        _____
        _____
        _____

What am I willing to sacrifice?

Who can I turn to for help?

Remember that you are actually helping a person feel good about him- or herself when you ask for their help. You're making their day!

What is my life ambition?

Your life ambition should be as short as possible, one or two sentences. You could also simply state from where and where to you want to move. Then you may always write several pages about the consequences.

HAPPINESS

8 How Do I Differentiate Myself from Others?

What am I better at than anybody else?

There are no limits to where you can go and what you can do. The only things that hold you back are your own self limitations. If you really believe that you're right, then go for it!

What else differentiates me from the rest?

There is value in diversity and what you contribute in a specific context is leveraged by the degree to which you are different.

How good do I want to be?

When you analyze new tasks or decisions always consider whether they contribute to your success criteria. Ask yourself: "What is in it for me?" The not urgent but important tasks and decisions are where value is created. Aim to dedicate at least 20% of your time to this Quadrant II.

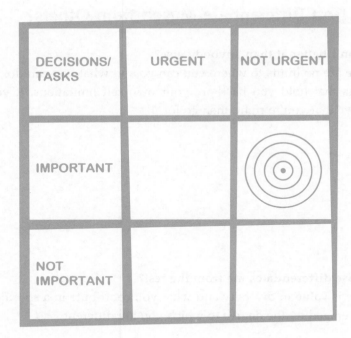

DECISIONS/ TASKS	URGENT	NOT URGENT
IMPORTANT		
NOT IMPORTANT		

My Quadrant II Tasks

9 What is My Personal Business Plan?

How can I reinvent myself in order to remain relevant?

If you were a brand, what would people say about you? What is your Personal Brand?

What is my BATNA (my Best Alternative to Negotiated Agreement)?

This gives you a benchmark with which to measure any future situation against your current situation. It protects you from accepting terms that are too unfavorable and rejecting terms that would be in your interest to accept.

Am I happy now?

If you are not happy now, you will never be happy! The ideal life is not free of challenges – you need to find the patterns in your life that are counterproductive and then change them!

10 What Have I Learned?

What is my time horizon?

Describe the journey from now to the optimal situation – from the perspective of the future situation and meaning and looking back. When you have imagined the future, all fear of it disappears.

How far can I go?

What would I attempt to do if I knew I could not fail?

Free yourself from the limitations created by your past. Look to the future and your best possible opportunity.

To infinity . . . and beyond!

NOTES

1 Kenneth P. De Meuse, *Proof Point: What's Smarter than IQ?* (Korn/Ferry International, 2012).

2 According to organizations and measures such as the OECD *Better Life Index*, *World Map of Happiness*, and *World Database of Happiness*. For examples of global happiness data, please go to oecdbetterlifeindex.org, mapofhappiness.com, or 1.eur.nl/fsw/happiness.

3 The quote is from an article (in Danish) about the Danish design firm Georg Jensen. *Berlingske Business Magasin*, November 15, 2012, p. 13.

4 BATNA is the standard against which any proposed plan should be measured. It is the only standard which can protect you from accepting terms that are too unfavorable as well as from rejecting terms it would be in your interest to accept. For more information on BATNA, please go to pon.harvard.edu/tag/batna/.

5 The Association for Executive Search Consultants (AESC) regularly surveys candidates and executive search consultants regarding career questions. For more information please go to aesc.org.

6 Named after John Venn, an English logician and philosopher. See John Venn, *Symbolic Logic* (1881) (Kessinger Publishing, 2007).

7 Claus Otto Scharmer, *Theory U: Leading from the Future as it Emerges* (Berrett-Koehler Publishers, 2007).

8 Pedersen, Vivi Bach Pedersen and Jeppesen, H. J., Contagious flexibility? A study on whether schedule flexibility facilitates work-life enrichment (*Scandinavian Journal of Psychology*, Under review).

9 Has led to the famous quote by Wayne Gretzky himself "I skate to where the puck is going to be, not where it is." The quote, and the idea of anticipating the future, has been widely adopted.

10 Much research on happiness underlines this point. Consider Professor Sonja Lyubomirsky of the University of California, Riverside, for example. An acolyte of David Seligman's and the author of *The How of Happiness: A Scientific Approach to Getting the Life You Want*, she contends that "a full 40 percent of the capacity for happiness is within your power to change."

11 David Lykken, Personality Similarity in Twins Reared Apart and Together (*Journal of Personality and Social Psychology*, Vol. 54, No. 6, 1988, pp. 1031–1039).

12 Carol Bartz talks about herself in Postcards – From the pinnacles of power by *Fortune* editor at large Patricia Sellers, *Yahoo CEO Carol Bartz: Unedited*, (*Fortune*, September 28, 2009). Read more at: http://postcards.blogs.fortune.cnn.com/ 2009/09/28/yahoo-ceo-carol-bartz-unedited/.

13 Reid Hoffman talks about his path from academia to social media in Alyssa Abkowitz's, How LinkedIn's founder got started, (*Fortune*, August 25, 2009). Read more:http://mutualfundsmag.us/2009/08/24/technologylinkedin_reid_hoffman. fortuneindex.htm.

14 Marcus Buckingham, *The One Thing You Need to Know . . . About Great Managing, Great Leading and Sustained Individual Success* (Free Press, 2005).

15 Hall, D. T, Self-awareness, identity and leader development. In D. V. Day, S. J. Zacaro, and S. M. Halpin (eds.), *Leader Development for Transforming Organizations: Growing Leaders for Tomorrow* (Lawrence Erlbaum Associates, 2004 pp. 153–176).

16 Edna St. Vincent Millay (1892–1950), US poet, *Childhood Is the Kingdom Where Nobody Dies* (1937).

17 Joseph Heller, *Catch-22* (Simon & Schuster, 1999).

18 For more information about this principle, refer to Marcus Buckingham, *The One Thing You Need to Know . . . About Great Managing, Great Leading and Sustained Individual Success* (Free Press, 2005).

19 At www.ccl.org/leadership/pdf/assessments/BMK_Sample_Feedback_Report.pdf, you will find a list of five potential career stallers: Problems with Interpersonal Relationships, Difficulty Building and Leading a Team, Difficulty Changing or Adapting, Failure to Meet Business Objectives and Too Narrow a Functional Orientation.

20 George Soros, The Man Who Cries Wolf, Now is Warning of a "Superbubble", (*The Wall Street Journal*, June 21, 2008). Read more: http://online.wsj.com/article/ SB121400427331093457.html#articleTabs%3Darticle.

21 For more information please visit insead.edu/mba.

22 Anne M. Mulcahy became CEO on Aug 1, 2001, Chairman on Jan 1, 2002 and announced her retirement as CEO on May 21, 2009 and as Chairman on May 20, 2010. The stock remained flat during the period. Anne M. Mulcahy was succeeded by Ursula Burns: "As I've progressed in my career, I've come to appreciate – and really value – the other attributes that define a company's success beyond the P&L: great leadership, long-term financial strength, ethical business practices, evolving business strategies, sound governance, powerful brands, values-based decision-making" *Ursula Burns, Chairman and CEO, Xerox Corporation.*

23 John Stuart Mill, *On Liberty* (Longman, Roberts and Green, 1869 and Bartleby.com, 1999).

24 Napoleon Hill (October 26, 1883 – November 8, 1970) was an American author widely considered to be one of the great writers on success.

25 Jeffrey Immelt is the Chairman and CEO of General Electric. GE's stock dropped from $60 in 2000 (when Immelt took the CEO position) to $19 in 2012. According

to *Reuters* (February 2009): "Jeffrey Immelt has waived his right to a bonus and performance-based pay that would have netted him more than $12 million in cash". This could be considered as a smart move, at least from the standpoint of public relations and shareholder sentiment.

26 Claus Otto Scharmer, *Theory U: Leading from the Future as it Emerges* (Berrett-Koehler Publishers, 2007, p. 164)

27 Andrew Weil, *Natural Remedies: Mother Nature's Little Helpers*, (Time.com, Monday, January 20, 2003) Read more: http://www.time.com/time/magazine/article/0,9171,1004085,00html#ixzz0YfnM9Ptb.

28 W. C. Fields (1880–1946) was an American comedian, actor, juggler and writer.

29 The theory of Situational Leadership was developed by Ken Blanchard, author of *The One Minute Manager*, and Paul Hersey, professor and author of the book *Situational Leader*. For further information see *Management of Organizational Behavior: Utilizing Human Resources*, by Blanchard and Hersey.

30 PAEI Management Styles were developed 30 years ago by Ichak Adizes. Read his book *The Ideal Executive* (Adizes Institute Publications, 2004) for more information on the framework.

31 Neil LaChapelle, *The Structure of Concern – A Challenge for Thinkers* (Lulu.com, 2008).

32 See myersbriggs.org/my-mbti-personality-type/mbti-basics/ for more information about the Myers-Briggs Type Indicator.

33 The *Belbin Team Roles* framework was developed by Meredith Belbin. See belbin.com for more information.

34 Association of Executive Search Consultants, *Executive Search and Your Career: The BlueSteps Guide to Career Management* (AESC, 2005).

35 Donald O. Clifton and Marcus Buckingham, *Now, Discover Your Strengths* (Free Press, 2001).

36 Marcus Buckingham, *Go Put Your Strengths to Work* (Free Press, 2007).

37 Prominent on Mr. Woodruff's desk was his personal creed: "There is no limit to what a man can do or where he can go if he doesn't mind who gets the credit".

38 Albert Camus (7 November 1913 – 4 January 1960) was a French author, philosopher and journalist who was awarded the Nobel Prize for Literature in 1957. He is often cited as a proponent of existentialism (the philosophy that he was associated with during his own lifetime), but Camus himself refused this particular label. In an interview in 1945, Camus rejected any ideological associations: "No, I am not an existentialist. Sartre and I are always surprised to see our names linked . . ."

39 Ram Charan, Ending the CEO Succession Crisis hbr.org/2005/02/ending-the-ceo-succession-crisis/ar/1: "And two out of every five new CEOs fail in the first 18 months, as Dan Ciampa cites in his article 'Almost Ready' in *Harvard Business Review*, January 2005".

40 Every year, Booz & Company takes a long and penetrating look at CEO succession among the world's top 2500 public companies. Their research goes back consecu-

tively to 2000, giving a good perspective on the tenure and position of these global business leaders. See for example www.booz.com/media/file/BoozCo-CEO-Succession-2010-Four-Types.pdf.

41 Reid Hoffman and Ben Casnocha, *The Start-up of You – Adapt to the Future, Invest in Yourself, and Transform Your Career* (Random House Business Books, 2012).

42 Richard R. Gesteland, *Cross-Cultural Business Behavior: Negotiating, Selling, Sourcing and Managing Across Cultures* (Copenhagen Business Press, 2005).

43 Sumantra Ghoshal and Christopher A. Bartlett, *Changing the Role of Top Management: Beyond Structure to Process* (Harvard Business Review, January – February 1995).

44 Jim Collins, *Built to Last: Successful Habits of Visionary Companies* (HarperBusiness, 1994).

45 Laura Nash and Howard Stephenson, *Just Enough: Tools for Creating Success in Your Work and Life* (John Wiley & Sons, Inc., 2004).

46 Robert S. Kaplan (born 1940) is co-creator, together with David P. Norton, of the balanced scorecard, a means of linking a company's current actions to its long-term goals. Kaplan and Norton introduced the balanced scorecard method in their 1992 *Harvard Business Review* article, "The Balanced Scorecard: Measures That Drive Performance".

47 Robert E. Kaplan and Robert B. Kaiser, *"Stop Overdoing Your Strengths"* (*Harvard Business Review*, February 2009).

48 Association of Executive Search Consultants, *Executive Search and Your Career: The BlueSteps Guide to Career Management* (AESC, 2005).

49 Said by Jim Crutchfield in a dialog between himself, Turbulent Landscape's scientific advisor, and Ned Kahn, its designer and curator – a scientist and an artist discussing the nature of patterns, the exhibits, and ways of seeing. Read more: http://cse.ucdavis.edu/~cmg/compmech/pubs/TurbLand.htm.

50 Howard Gardner, *Frames of Mind: The Theory of Multiple Intelligences* (Basic Books, 1983).

51 "I have most almost invariably found that the very feeling which has seemed to me most private, most personal, and hence most incomprehensible by others, has turned out to be an expression for which there is a resonance in many other people . . ." Carl Rogers, *On Becoming a Person: A Therapist's View of Psychotherapy* (Houghton Mifflin, 1989, p. 26).

52 Rudolf Steiner, reference to several seminal works.

53 Thomas Hobbes of Malmesbury (5 April 1588 – 4 December 1679) was an English philosopher, best known today for his work on political philosophy. His 1651 book *Leviathan* established the foundation for most of Western political philosophy from the perspective of social contract theory. Chapter XIII contains what has been called one of the best-known passages in English philosophy, which describes the natural state mankind would be in, were it not for political community: "Whatsoever therefore is consequent to a time of war, where every man is enemy to every man; the same is consequent to the time, wherein men live without other security, than what

their own strength, and their own invention shall furnish them withal. In such condition, there is no place for industry; because the fruit thereof is uncertain: and consequently no culture of the earth; no navigation, nor use of the commodities that may be imported by sea; no commodious building; no instruments of moving, and removing, such things as require much force; no knowledge of the face of the earth; no account of time; no arts; no letters; no society; and which is worst of all, continual fear, and danger of violent death; and the life of man, solitary, poor, *nasty, brutish, and short.*"

54 Paul Arden, *It's Not How Good You Are, It's How Good You Want To Be* (Phaidon Press Limited, 2003).

55 Robert Kegan, *In Over Our Heads: The Mental Demands of Modern Life* (Harvard University Press, 2000).

56 *The Economist*, "Age and Happiness: The U-bend of Life" (December 16, 2010) www.economist.com/node/17722567.

57 Malcolm Gladwell, *Outliers: The Story of Success* (Little, Brown, 2008).

58 An old Indian proverb has it like this: *If you want to criticize a person, start walking five miles in his moccasins.*

59 Richard Branson, *Business Stripped Bare – Adventures Of A Global Entrepreneur* (St. Martin's Press, 2008).

60 Reid Hoffman and Ben Casnocha, *The Start-up of You – Adapt to the Future, Invest in Yourself, and Transform Your Career* (Random House Business Books, 2012).

61 John Kotter, *Leading Change* (Harvard Business School Press, 1996).

62 Henry David Thoreau, in his conclusion to *Walden*: "I learned this, at least, by my experiment: that if one *advances confidently in the direction of his dreams, and endeavors to live the life which he has imagined,* he will meet with a success unexpected in common hours. He will put some things behind, will pass an invisible boundary; new, universal, and more liberal laws will begin to establish themselves around and within him; or the old laws be expanded, and interpreted in his favor in a more liberal sense, and he will live with the license of a higher order of beings. In proportion as he simplifies his life, the laws of the universe will appear less complex, and solitude will not be solitude, nor poverty poverty, nor weakness weakness. If you have built castles in the air, your work need not be lost; that is where they should be. Now put the foundations under them."

63 The first Ferris wheel was designed by George W. Ferris, a bridge-builder from Pittsburgh, Pennsylvania. He built the Ferris Wheel for the 1893 World's Fair, which was held in Chicago to commemorate the 400th anniversary of Columbus' landing in America.

64 Gene O'Kelly, chairman and chief executive of KPMG International, died of brain cancer September 10, 2004. In the 100 days between he was diagnosed and his death, he wrote the book, *Chasing Daylight: How My Forthcoming Death Transformed My Life.*

65 Patricia Sellers, *"Indra Nooyi is the Queen of Pop"* (*Fortune*, September 10, 2009). Read more: http://money.cnn.com/2009/09/09/news/companies/pepsico_indra_nooyi_ceo.fortune/index.htm.

66 Martin Seligman, *Authentic Happiness: Using the New Positive Psychology to Realize Your Potential for Lasting Fulfillment* (Free Press, 2002).

67 As the Greek philosopher Diogenes (about 412–323 BC) pointed out: "Dogs and philosophers are those who do most good and are rewarded worst".

68 Mihaly Csikszentmihalyi, *Flow: The Psychology of Optimal Experience* (Harper and Row, 1990).

69 Great men in history who suffered from depression are numerous: Abraham Lincoln, Ernest Hemingway, Winston Churchill and Buzz Aldrin to name a few. Buzz Aldrin overcame his depression and alcoholism, eventually becoming Chair of the National Mental Health Association. Churchill took up painting to keep what he called the "black dog" at bay.

70 "Rhetorical power", wrote Churchill, "is neither wholly bestowed, nor wholly acquired, but cultivated."

71 For more information on Dr. Seligman's School of Positive Psychology and free use of self testing instruments please refer to authentichappiness.sas.upenn.edu.

72 Claudia Wallis, *"The New Science of Happiness"* (*Time* Magazine, Time.com, Sunday, January 9, 2005). Read more: time.com/time/magazine/article/0,9171,1015902-1,00.html.

73 Richard Corliss, *"Staying Healthy: Is There a Formula For Joy?"* (*Time* Magazine, Time.com, Monday, January 20, 2003). Read more: time.com/time/magazine/article/0,9171,1004095-1,00.html and Dan Baker, *What Happy People Know: How the New Science of Happiness Can Change Your Life for the Better* (St. Martin's Press, 2004).

74 Pete Cohen and Carol Rothwel, *Happiness is No Laughing Matter* (Happiness Report, January 2003).

75 Edward Diener (born 1946) is an American psychologist, professor, and author. He is noted for his fundamental research on happiness over the past more than 25 years and is nicknamed *Dr. Happiness*.

76 David Lykken, "Personality Similarity in Twins Reared Apart and Together" (*Journal of Personality and Social Psychology*, Vol. 54, No. 6, 1988, pp. 1031–1039).

77 Edward Diener, "Reexamining Adaptation and the Set Point Model of Happiness: Reactions to Changes in Marital Status" (*Journal of Personality and Social Psychology*, Vol. 84, No. 3, 2003, pp. 527–539).

78 Sandra Murray, John G. Holmes, Dan Dolderman, and Dale W. Griffin, "What the Motivated Mind Sees: Comparing Friends' Perspectives to Married Partners' Views of Each Other" (Academic Press, *Journal of Experimental Social Psychology*, Vol. 36, November 2000, pp. 600–620).

79 Ambrose Bierce, *The Devil's Dictionary*, (Oxford University Press, 1999).

80 Tor Norretranders, *Rejoice* (TV2, 2007) (In Danish). See edge.org for more information.

81 Alice M. Isen, And U. Turken and F. Gregory Ashby, "A Neuropsychological Theory of Positive Affect and Its Influence on Cognition" (*Psychological Review*, Vol. 106, No. 3, 1999, pp. 529–550).

82 Wolfram Schultz has made contributions to our understanding of the reward functions of dopamine neurons and of neurons in other parts of the brain's reward system. He has also done important work on the relationship between reward and risk information in the brain, especially in relation to learning theory and neuroeconomics.

83 Timothy Butler, *Getting Unstuck: How Dead Ends Become New Paths*, (Harvard Business School Press, 2007).

84 Roberto C. Goizueta, the renowned former CEO of The Coca-Cola Company, said that when concentrating deeply on some task at hand, he developed a sweat.

85 Richard Branson, *Business Stripped Bare – Adventures Of A Global Entrepreneur* (St. Martin's Press, 2008).

86 J. Evelyn Orr, *Becoming an Agile Leader – A Guide to Learning From Your Experiences*, (Lominger International: A Korn/Ferry Company, 2012).

87 Victoria V. Swisher, *Becoming an Agile Leader – Know What to Do . . . when you don't know what to do*, (Lominger International: A Korn/Ferry Company, 2012).

88 Jim Collins, *Good to Great: Why Some Companies Make the Leap . . . and Others Don't* (HarperBusiness, 2001).

89 Association of Executive Search Consultants, *Executive Search and Your Career: The BlueSteps Guide to Career Management* (AESC, 2005).

90 Mark Albion, *Making a Life, Making a Living: Reclaiming Your Purpose and Passion in Business and in Life*, (Warner Business Books, 2000).

91 Rob Cross and Andrew Parker, *The Hidden Power of Social Networks: Understanding How Work Really Gets Done in Organizations* (Harvard Business Press, 2004).

92 Alpha waves, along with beta waves, were discovered by German neurologist Hans Berger, most famous for his invention of the electroencephalography (EEG).

93 Richard Tomlinson, *L'Oréal's Global Makeover: How did a Brit from Liverpool turn an emblem of French chic into an international star? One brand at a time* (September 30, 2002) Read more: http://money.cnn.com/magazines/fortune/fortune_archive/2002/09/30/329290/index.htm.

94 Daniel Roth, "Can Nike Still Do It Without Phil Knight?" (*Fortune*, April 4, 2005) Read more: http://money.cnn.com/magazines/fortune/fortune_archive/2005/04/04/8255930/index.htm.

95 Geoff Colvin, *Talent Is Overrated: What Really Separates World-Class Performers From Everybody Else* (Penguin Books, 2008).

96 Kurt Badenhausen, *Sports' First Billion-Dollar Man*, (Forbes.com 29 September, 2009) forbes.com/2009/09/29/tiger-woods-billion-business-sports-tiger.html.

97 Malcolm Gladwell, *Outliers: The Story of Success* (Little, Brown, 2008).

98 Robert W. Weisberg discusses the Beatles – and computes the hours they spent practicing – in *Creativity and Knowledge: A Challenge to Theories, in Handbook of Creativity*, (ed. Robert J. Sternberg) (Cambridge University Press, 1999).

99 For more information on the 10 000-hour rule, please refer to the original inventors of the concept K. Anders Ericsson, Ralf Th. Krampe, and Clemens Tesch-Romer, The Role of Deliberate Practice in the Acquisition of Expert Performance (*Psychological Review*, Vol. 100, No. 3, 1993, 363–406). Daniel J. Levitin talks about the 10 000 hours it takes to get mastery in *This is Your Brain on Music: The Science of a Human Obsession* (Dutton, 2006, p. 197).

100 Carlos Castaneda, *Teachings of Don Juan: A Yaqui Way of Knowledge*, (Simon & Schuster Adult, 1985).

101 Used with permission of Nike www.nike.com.

102 Association of Executive Search Consultants, *Executive Search and Your Career: The BlueSteps Guide to Career Management* (AESC, 2005).

103 Please find more details about Paul Evans's Egg Model in the following presentation http://miyaichi.up.seesaa.net/image/PrC3A6sentation20poul20evans.pdf.

104 Thomas Kuhn (1922–1996) is the author of *The Structure of Scientific Revolutions* from 1962 where the terms paradigm and paradigm shift were popularized.

105 Stephen R. Covey, *The 7 Habits of Highly Effective People* (Free Press, 1990).

106 Stephen R. Covey, *First Things First* (Free Press, 1996).

107 Stig Rossen is a Danish actor and vocalist.

108 The article, "The Man Who Invented Management – Why Peter Drucker's Ideas Still Matter" (*Business Week*, November 28, 2005) is an interesting article about Peter Drucker and how he contributed to the business world and the world of management. Read more: businessweek.com/magazine/content/05_48/b3961001.htm.

109 Gary Hamel, *Leading the Revolution* (Harvard Business School Press, 2000).

110 Howard Gardner, *Frames of Mind: The Theory of Multiple Intelligences* (Basic Books, 1983).

111 Roger Fisher and William Ury, *Getting to Yes: Negotiating Agreement Without Giving In* (Penguin Books, 1991).

112 Richard Branson, *Business Stripped Bare – Adventures of a Global Entrepreneur* (St. Martin's Press, 2008).

113 Bronnie Ware, *The Top Five Regrets of the Dying: A Life Transformed by the Dearly Departing* (Hay House, 2011).

114 Stephen M. R. Covey, *The Speed of Trust, The One Thing that Changes Everything* (Free Press, 2006).

115 W. Chan Kim and Renée Mauborgne, *Blue Ocean Strategy* (Harvard Business School Press, 2005).

116 Eric Ries, *The Lean Startup* (Crown Business, 2011).

117 Ralph D. Stacey, *Complex Responsive Processes in Organizations* (Routledge, 2001).

118 Jason Fried and David Heinemeier Hansson, *Rework* (Crown Business, 2010).

TOP 10 RECOMMENDED READING

The leadership literature is overwhelming. It can be separated into two traditions:

- ⊗ The Troubadour Tradition: Opinions of self-appointed gurus and former CEOs
- ⊗ The Academic Tradition: Empirical research from Academia

The Troubadour Tradition is entertaining but unscientific. The Academic Tradition is scientific but often trivial. In this Top 10 I have tried to accommodate both schools of thought and picked representative works. By reading these books and applying the insights you will become a happier person and a better leader.

1. Buckingham, Marcus, *The One Thing You Need to Know . . . About Great Managing, Great Leading and Sustained Individual Success*, Free Press, 2005.
2. Coelho, Paulo, *The Alchemist*, HarperCollins, 1993.
3. Covey, Stephen M. R., *The Speed of Trust, The One Thing that Changes Everything*, Free Press, 2006.
4. Hamel, Gary, *What Matters Now – How to Win in a World of Relentless Change, Ferocious Competition, and Unstoppable Innovation*, Jossey-Bass, 2012.
5. Magretta, Joan, *What Management Is: How it Works and Why it's Everyone's Business*, HarperCollinsBusiness, 2002.
6. Mintzberg, Henry, Bruce Ahlstrand and Joseph Lampel, *Strategy Safari: A Guided Tour Through the Wilds of Strategic Management*, Free Press, 1998.
7. Scharmer, Claus Otto, *Theory U – Leading from the Future as It Emerges*, Berrett-Koehler Publishers, 2007.
8. Schein, Edgar H., *Organizational Culture and Leadership*, Jossey-Bass, 1992.
9. Seligman, Martin, *Authentic Happiness: Using the New Positive Psychology to Realize Your Potential for Lasting Fulfillment*, Free Press, 2002.
10. Yalom, Irvin D., *Existential Psychotherapy*, Yalom Family Trust, 1980.

BIBLIOGRAPHY

Abell, Derek F., *Managing With Dual Strategies, Mastering the Present, Preempting the Future* (Free Press, 1993).

Adizes, Ichak, *The Ideal Executive* (Adizes Institute Publications, 2004).

Albion, Mark, *Making a Life, Making a Living: Reclaiming Your Purpose and Passion in Business and in Life* (Warner Business Books, 2000).

Arden, Paul, *It's Not How Good You Are, It's How Good You Want To Be* (Phaidon Press Limited, 2003).

Argyris, Chris and Donald Schön, *Organizational Learning: A Theory of Action Perspective* (Addison Wesley, 1978).

Association of Executive Search Consultants, *Executive Search and Your Career (The BlueSteps Guide to Career Management)* (AESC, 2005).

Baker, Dan, *What Happy People Know – How the New Science of Happiness can Change Your Life for the Better* (St. Martin's Press, 2004).

Barnett, William P., *The Red Queen among Organizations: How Competitiveness Evolves* (Princeton University Press, 2008).

Bierce, Ambrose, *The Devil's Dictionary* (Oxford University Press, 1999).

Blanchard, Ken and Paul Hersey, *Management of Organizational Behavior: Utilizing Human Resources* (Prentice Hall, 2001).

Bogsnes, Bjarte, *Implementing Beyond Budgeting – Unlocking the Performance Potential* (John Wiley & Sons, Inc., 2009).

Branson, Richard, *Business Stripped Bare – Adventures of a Global Entrepreneur* (St. Martin's Press, 2008).

Brousseau, Kenneth R., Driver, Michael J., Hourihan, Gary and Larsson, Rikard, *The Seasoned Executive's Decision-Making Style*, based on proprietary research from Korn/ Ferry International (Harvard Business Review, February 2006).

Bruyant-Langer, Stephen, *Your Next Career – The Headhunter's Guide to Lifelong Success* (In Danish) (Lindhardt & Ringhof, 2012).

Bruyant-Langer, Stephen, *The Competition Concept of the Future – An Epochal Theory* (In Danish) (Leadership Today, 1999).

Buckingham, Marcus, *Go Put Your Strengths to Work* (Free Press, 2007).

Buckingham, Marcus, *The One Thing You Need to Know . . . About Great Managing, Great Leading and Sustained Individual Success* (Free Press, 2005).

Butler, Timothy, *Getting Unstuck: How Dead Ends Become New Paths* (Harvard Business School Press, 2007).

Camus, Albert, *The Fall* (Vintage Books, 1991).

Castaneda, Carlos, *Teachings of Don Juan: A Yaqui Way of Knowledge* (Simon & Schuster Adult, 1985).

Charan, Ram, *Ending the CEO Succession Crisis* (*Harvard Business Review*, February 2005).

Clifton, Donald O. and Marcus Buckingham, *Now, Discover Your Strengths* (Free Press, 2001).

Coelho, Paulo, *The Alchemist* (HarperCollins, 1993).

Cohen, Pete and Carol Rothwel, *Happiness is No Laughing Matter* (*Happiness Report*, January 2003).

Collins, Jim, Good to Great: *Why Some Companies Make the Leap . . . and Others Don't* (HarperBusiness, 2001).

Collins, Jim, Built to Last: *Successful Habits of Visionary Companies* (HarperBusiness, 1994).

Colvin, Geoff, *Talent Is Overrated: What Really Separates World-Class Performers From Everybody Else* (Penguin Books, 2008).

Covey, Stephen M. R., *The Speed of Trust, The One Thing that Changes Everything* (Free Press, 2006).

Covey, Stephen M. R., *The 7 Habits of Highly Effective People* (Free Press, 1990).

Cooperrider, David and Suresh Srivastva, Appreciative Inquiry In Organizational Life, in *Research In Organization Change and Development* (*JAI Press* Vol. 1, 1987, pp. 129–169).

Cross, Rob and Andrew Parker, *The Hidden Power of Social Networks: Understanding How Work Really Gets Done in Organizations* (Harvard Business Press, 2004).

Csikszentmihalyi, Mihaly, *Flow: The Psychology of Optimal Experience* (Harper and Row, 1990).

De Meuse, Kenneth P., *What's Smarter than IQ?* (Korn/Ferry Institute, October 2011).

Diener, Edward, Reexamining Adaptation and the Set Point Model of Happiness: Reactions to Changes in Marital Status (*Journal of Personality and Social Psychology*, Vol. 84, No. 3, 2003, pp. 527–539).

Drucker, Peter, *The Effective Executives (1966)* (HarperCollins Publishers, 1993).

Ericsson, K. Anders, Ralf Th. Krampe, and Clemens Tesch-Romer, The Role of Deliberate Practice in the Acquisition of Expert Performance (*Psychological Review*, Vol. 100, No. 3, 1993, pp. 363–406).

Fisher, Roger and William Ury, *Getting to Yes: Negotiating Agreement without Giving In* (Penguin Books, 1991).

Fried, Jason and David Heinemeier Hansson, *Rework* (Crown Business, 2010).

Fukuyama, Francis, *Trust* (Free Press, 1995).

Gardner, Howard, *Frames of Mind: The Theory of Multiple Intelligences* (Basic Books, 1983).

Gesteland, Richard R., *Cross-Cultural Business Behavior: Negotiating, Selling, Sourcing and Managing Across Cultures* (Copenhagen Business Press, 2005).

Ghoshal, Sumantra and Christopher A. Bartlett, *Changing the Role of Top Management: Beyond Structure to Process* (*Harvard Business Review*, January–February 1995).

Gladwell, Malcolm, *Outliers, The Story of Success* (Little, Brown, 2008).

Goleman, Daniel, *Working with Emotional Intelligence* (Bantam, 1998).

Goleman, Daniel, Richard Boyatzis, and Annie McKee, *Primal Leadership: Realizing the Power of Emotional Intelligence* (Harvard Business Press, 2002).

Hamel, Gary, *Leading the Revolution*, (Harvard Business School Press, 2000).

Hamel, Gary, Management 2:0 (*Wall Street Journal* blog, 2009).

Hamel, Gary and Bill Breen, *The Future of Management* (Harvard Business School Press, 2007).

Hamel, Gary, *What Matters Now – How to Win in a World of Relentless Change, Ferocious Competition, and Unstoppable Innovation* (Jossey-Bass, 2012).

Hamilton, Stewart and Alicia Micklethwait, *Greed and Corporate Failure: The Lessons from Recent Disasters* (Palgrave Macmillan, 2006).

Harter, James K., Frank L. Schmidt, and Theodore L. Hayes, Business Unit-Level Relationship between Employee Satisfaction, Employee Engagement and Business Outcomes: A Meta Analysis (*Journal of Applied Psychology*, Vol. 87, 2002, pp. 268–279).

Heller, Joseph, *Catch-22* (Simon & Schuster, 1999).

Hildebrandt, Steen, *From Local Optimization to Global Responsibility* (In Danish) (2008).

Hoffman, Reid and Ben Casnocha, *The Start-up of You – Adapt to the Future, Invest in Yourself, and Transform Your Career* (Random House Business Books, 2012).

Hogan, Robert, John A. Johnson, and Stephen R. Briggs, *Handbook of Personality Psychology* (Gulf Professional Publishing, 1997).

Isaacson, Walter, *Steve Jobs* (Little, Brown, 2011).

Isen, Alice M., And U. Turken, and F. Gregory Ashby, A Neuropsychological Theory of Positive Affect and Its Influence on Cognition (*Psychological Review*, Vol. 106, No. 3, 1999, pp. 529–550).

Jensen, Jesper Bo, Anne-Marie Dahl, Kristine Baastrup, Tine Schack-Nielsen, Martin Riise Nielsen, and Line Urban, *The Consumer's Journey into the Future* (2000, unpublished research paper).

Judge, Timothy A., Joyce E. Bono, Remus Ilies, and Megan Gerhardt, Personality and Leadership: A Qualitative and Quantitative Review (*Journal of Applied Psychology*, Vol. 87, No. 4, 2002, pp. 765–780).

Kanter, Rosabeth Moss, *America the Principled* (Random House, 2007).

Kaplan Robert E. and Robert B. *Kaiser, Stop Overdoing Your Strengths* (*Harvard Business Review*, February 2009).

Kaplan, Robert S., Anthony A. Atkinson, Ella Mae Matsumura, and S. Mark Young, *Management Accounting. 5th edn.* (Pearson Prentice Hall, 2007).

Kegan, Robert, *In Over Our Heads* (Harvard University Press, 2000).

Kim, W. Chan and Renée Mauborgne, *Blue Ocean Strategy* (Harvard Business School Press, 2005).

Kotter, John, *Leading Change* (Harvard Business School Press, 1996).

Kuhn, Thomas, *The Structure of Scientific Revolutions* (University of Chicago Press, 1962).

LaChapelle, Neil, *The Structure of Concern – A Challenge for Thinkers* (Lulu.com, 2008).

Levitin, Daniel J., *This is Your Brain on Music: The Science of a Human Obsession* (Dutton, 2006).

Levitt Steven D. and Stephen J. Dubner, *Freakonomics: A Rogue Economist Explores the Hidden Side of Everything* (HarperCollins, 2005).

Lindstrom, Martin, *Buyology, Truth and Lies about Why We Buy* (Random House, 2008).

Lykken, David, Personality Similarity in Twins Reared Apart and Together (*Journal of Personality and Social Psychology*, Vol. 54, No. 6, 1988, pp. 1031–1039).

Lyubomirsky, Sonja, *The How of Happiness: A Scientific Approach to Getting the Life You Want* (Penguin Press, 2007).

Magretta, Joan, *What Management Is: How it Works and Why it's Everyone's Business* (HarperCollinsBusiness, 2002).

Meredith, Robyn, *The Elephant and the Dragon – The Rise of India and China and What It Means for All of Us* (W. W. Norton & Company, 2007).

Mintzberg, Henry, Bruce Ahlstrand, and Joseph Lampel, *Strategy Safari: A Guided Tour Through the Wilds of Strategic Management* (Free Press, 1998).

Murray, Sandra, John G. Holmes, Dan Dolderman, and Dale W. Griffin, What the Motivated Mind Sees: Comparing Friends' Perspectives to Married Partners' Views of Each Other (Academic Press, *Journal of Experimental Social Psychology*, Vol. 36, November 2000, pp. 600–620).

Nash, Laura and Howard Stephenson, *Just Enough: Tools for Creating Success in Your Work and Life* (John Wiley & Sons, Inc., 2004).

Norretranders, Tor, *Rejoice* (In Danish) (2007).

O'Kelly, Gene, *Chasing Daylight: How My Forthcoming Death Transformed My Life* (McGraw-Hill, 2006).

Orr, J. Evelyn, *Becoming an Agile Leader – A Guide to Learning From Your Experiences* (Lominger International – A Korn/Ferry Company, 2012).

Pirzig, Robert M., *Zen and the Art of Motorcycle Maintenance* (Bantam Books, 1984).

Ries, Eric, *The Lean Startup* (Crown Business, 2011).

Ritskes, Rients, *The Zen Manager* (In Danish) (Self-published, 2000).

Ritskes, Rients and Merel Ritske-Holtinga, *Endorphins: How To Produce Your Own Happiness Hormones* (In Danish) (Bogan, 2001).

Rogers, Carl, *On Becoming a Person: A Therapist's View of Psychotherapy* (Houghton Mifflin, 1989).

Scharmer, Claus Otto, *Theory U – Leading from the Future as It Emerges* (Berrett-Koehler Publishers, 2007).

Schein, Edgar H., *Organizational Culture and Leadership* (Jossey-Bass, 1992).

Seligman, Martin, *Authentic Happiness: Using the New Positive Psychology to Realize Your Potential for Lasting Fulfillment* (Free Press, 2002).

Stacey, Ralph D., Complex Responsive Processes in Organizations (Routledge, 2001).

Swisher, Victoria V., *Becoming an Agile Leader – Know What to Do . . . When You Don't Know What to Do* (Lominger International – A Korn/Ferry Company, 2012).

Venn, John, *Symbolic Logic (1881)* (Kessinger Publishing, 2007).

Ware, Bronnie, *The Top Five Regrets of the Dying: A Life Transformed by the Dearly Departing* (Hay House, 2011).

Watkins, Michael, *The First 90 Days: Critical Success Strategies for New Leaders at All Levels* (Harvard Business Press, 2003).

Welch, Jack with Suzy Welch, *Winning – The Ultimate Business How-To Book* (HarperCollins, 2005).

Weisberg, Robert W., Creativity and Knowledge: A Challenge to Theories, in: *Handbook of Creativity*, (ed. Robert J. Sternberg) (Cambridge University Press, 1999).

Wilkinson, David J., *The Ambiguity Advantage, What Great Leaders Are Great At* (Palgrave Macmillan, 2006).

Yalom, Irvin D., *Existential Psychotherapy* (Yalom Family Trust, 1980).

ABOUT THE AUTHOR

Stephen Bruyant-Langer is a senior partner with Korn/Ferry International, the world's leading Executive Search and Talent Management firm. He has successfully transformed the lives of hundreds of top-level executives through his world-class Executive Coaching Program. For more than 15 years, he worked as a Marketing Executive for global market leaders such as L'Oréal and The Coca-Cola Company before reinventing himself as a Headhunter and Executive Coach in 1996.

For more than 17 years he has in parallel pursued an academic career as an External Lecturer at Copenhagen Business School, focusing on Strategic Market Management and Corporate Communication. He has published more than 400 articles and columns on leadership and is widely used as a keynote speaker at conferences. In March 2012, he published his Danish best-selling leadership book *Your Next Career – the Headhunter's Guide to Lifelong Success.*

Stephen Bruyant-Langer is happily married to Mette, who is a Vice President in a publicly listed company. Together they have four grown-up children. The family lives in Denmark, near the sea and the forest. He has dual French/Danish citizenship, has lived in Belgium, France and Denmark, and is fluent in English, French, and Danish.

INDEX

Index compiled by Terry Halliday